ELEMENTARY
Following Jesus Strong and Simple

BEN PASLEY

Blue Renaissance Publishing

Published by Blue Renaissance Publishing
743 Gold Hill Place
Woodland Park, CO 80863

Cover Design: Kent Jensen, www.knail.com
Edited By: Angie West
Printed in the Unites States of America
ISBN: 978-0-9825434-8-1
Library of Congress Control Number: 2014918864

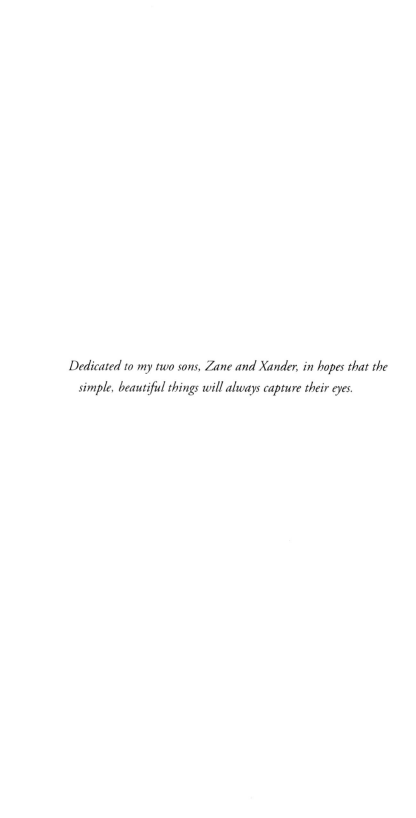

Dedicated to my two sons, Zane and Xander, in hopes that the simple, beautiful things will always capture their eyes.

TABLE OF CONTENTS

A KINGDOM FOR EVERYONE

It was to ordinary people, just like you and I, that Jesus said, "Follow me." As he walked along the country roads of Galilee he invited everyday people into relationship with him. He spoke plain words to plain people—like fisherman, accountants, and housewives, so, best I can tell, he still speaks plain words to us today. He seems to be picking us out one at a time—plain, everyday folks—and asking us to follow him. Jesus does not offer a complex system of beliefs and rituals. He offers us a very simple path to a new life with him.

One time, in the Bible's account of Jesus' life, caring parents were bringing their kids to Jesus so he could touch them and pray for them. He loved spending time with children. They were gathering around him in a public place, but some of his close followers became annoyed because they wanted to move on to bigger and better things. Jesus said to them, "Let the children come to me. Don't stop them! For the Kingdom of God belongs to those who are like these children. I tell you the truth, anyone who doesn't receive the Kingdom of God like a child will never enter it" (Luke 18:16–17). This helps me to believe that I can follow him, too. Access to his Kingdom, he said, does not require a complicated decision process, but the simplicity of a childlike trust.

Jesus spent a lot of time describing the Kingdom that he wanted to lead us into, and it is definitely a place I would like to go. In his Kingdom, relational intimacy is the norm, people always honor one another, weak people are never overlooked, and he always has a hand of friendship resting on our shoulders. His Kingdom is stable and secure, and he said it would last forever. Thankfully, his Kingdom is more personal than it is political, and God has invited every one of us to come into it.

Jesus once had a conversation with a very smart man on exactly how to enter the Kingdom. This man was a leader in religious things, and he had already spent much of his life studying the Old Testament scriptures, but Jesus explained the childlike simplicity of entering the Kingdom once again. Jesus said to Nicodemus in John 3, "I tell you the truth, unless you are born again, you cannot see the Kingdom of God" (John 3:3). This simple requirement removed Nicodemus from advanced placement because of his intellect or religious resume. This moment stands as a relief for all of us. What Jesus requires of us to enter his Kingdom puts us all on the same level. Jesus said we must become infants in the hands of God to enter the Kingdom —we have to be born again.

In the famous passage John 3:16, which was just a little later in their conversation, Jesus explained to Nicodemus, "For God loved the world so much that he gave his one and only Son, so that everyone who believes in him will not perish but have eternal life." This, the most well known verse in all the Bible, contains only childlike themes: love, gifts, trust, and dreams for the future. Nicodemus was a teachable teacher, and I think that is why Jesus took time to explain the Kingdom to him. Children are teachable as well, and I think that is why Jesus loved to spend so much time with them. To receive the simplicity of Jesus' invitation to follow him requires each of us to have a teachable, childlike heart. Christianity is not a culture of activities and meetings, or intellectual arguments and philosophy. When we decide to follow

2

Christ we are miraculously born again into his family as trusting children beginning a brand new life.

Children see everything through the lens of relationships and trust, and this is how we can best understand following Jesus into his Kingdom. It is certainly how Jesus understood it when he prayed, "O Father, Lord of heaven and earth, thank you for hiding these things from those who think themselves wise and clever, and for revealing them to the childlike. Yes, Father, it pleased you to do it this way!" (Matthew 11:25–26). Children learn simple things, and then they apply their simple conclusions to life. They come up with the best insights about things we often overlook as adults, because children don't make anything more complex than it should be. My son, Zane, when he was only about four years old was already solving important physical engineering issues. He was holding a banana, admiring its curved shape, about to take a bite, when he exclaimed, "I know why bananas are shaped like this!"

"Why, Zane?" we asked.

He sat up tall in his chair, and leaned way over the table and over the banana without moving his hand or the banana. Then, while he was demonstrating how he would have to bite it if it were sticking straight up at the ceiling, he said, "So we don't have to eat it like this!"

My wife and I laughed for quite a while thinking about straight bananas and all the kids in the world who would choose not to tilt their hands, but instead contort themselves into the most awkward positions to eat these difficult, straight bananas that were never pointing, conveniently, at their mouths. Zane was so proud of his discovery. Today, my son still loves solving engineering problems, and even though he is a young teenager, his best solutions continue to be built on the simplest of facts.

God's solutions for our lives are built on the simplest of facts as well. When we choose to follow Christ we will learn that simple things are the way of his Kingdom.

A KINGDOM OF REST

In my own journey following Jesus, which began when I was about eleven years old, I have had some very high and some very low points. When I look back over my life, however, I can see a long, certain progress toward a healthy place with God. It has not been easy, or perfect, but what makes it better is that I have not been alone. I have learned that following Jesus is not a journey where I am always ten miles, or even ten steps, behind him. He lets me walk right beside him, and he keeps a hand on my shoulder.

I did not understand this invitation to a close friendship with Jesus when I first started following him. I became so tired, at a very young age, of trying to please God. I was always running to catch up to his standards. My legs grew tired trying to cover the distance between us, and I felt very alone. Christianity, itself, seemed disappointed in me. Much of my religious experience seemed intent on reminding me that I was not quite there yet.

This is not how Jesus meant for me to hear his words. This is not how how he thinks about our journey together. We were having a serious communication problem. Speaking of communication problems, I am reminded of my relationship with my wife, Robin, when she has had to remind me: "You heard my words, but you are not hearing my heart!" I have sometimes put wrong meanings to words that she said to me because I had made judgments before she even began to speak. Many of us have problems like this when we first hear Jesus speak to us. Many of us have problems even entering this conversation because we have so many judgments against Christians, Christianity, or sometimes, even, ourselves.

I must admit, embarrassingly, that many people's first impressions of Christianity are ruined by people just like me when I was so full of striving toward God. Many people see Christians just like me, and watch our lonely, painful pursuit of unattainable perfection and they say to themselves, no way. My life was painting Christianity to be an unrealistic, burdensome call to conform to an impossible standard. This is why so many view Christianity as a kind of self-destructive prison that only self-haters and the pathologically guilty would ever enter.

That is not how Jesus invites us to walk with him. This is not how he wants us to feel about ourselves. He always speaks of us in the most caring ways and he is committed, eternally, to our well being. There was a point in my life, through a series of events and Divine encounters, where I caught a glimpse of Jesus in a new light. I began to hear his words in a new way. I heard him—I mean I heard him from the heart—say, "Come to me, all of you who are weary and carry heavy burdens, and I will give you rest. Take my yoke upon you. Let me teach you, because I am humble and gentle at heart, and you will find rest for your souls. For my yoke is easy to bear, and the burden I give you is light" Matthew 11:28–30.

Jesus is completely sincere. He means exactly what he says. There is no sarcasm in him. Jesus wants us to rest from striving toward our view of perfection, and be close to him instead. He wants us to be born again into a brand new life with him, and to grow up strong and healthy as well. His invitation is for us to come away from loneliness and tiredness, because he has a better place for us that is full of friendship and strength! The journey toward our friendship with God will not require us to run in order to catch up with him, because he will walk beside us. He has a very specific destination in mind so we will have to submit to his leadership, but his leadership is so kind and so loving. When Jesus asks each of us, "Follow me," he means exactly what he is saying. We must choose to trust that following him is better than simply waving at him from a distance, and our safety, our very lives, are dependent on a simple, childlike trust.

A KINGDOM OF MEANING

Mr. Rogers made a profound impression on me when I was a young boy. His show was strange, his puppets unsophisticated, but his kind, soft manner was so attractive to me. I could lay on the floor in front of the old TV set and let those silly-simple songs and his gentle words of encouragement just wash over me. It is nice to be loved, and it is nice to be spoken to with kindness. I believe this way of kindness was birthed in Fred Rogers, an ordained Presbyterian minister, through his relationship with Jesus.

Recently, I watched a documentary about Fred Rogers and his amazing career as the founding force behind the longest running show in Public Television's history. He said to the director of the documentary in their first meeting, "I feel so strongly that deep and simple is far more essential than shallow and complex." This was said so personally, and it had such impact on the director, that this sentence became the source of the documentary's title and premise. This sentence also sums up the nature of this book. If Jesus said that entering the Kingdom of God requires each of us to be childlike in our approach, then I believe we must apply that principle to everything else in our spiritual lives. We must dig down past the complexity and noise of this world and find the simple, valuable things to build our lives on. We must fight past the avalanche of religious trivia in this world to see the few really important things. We will discover there are not that many things at the deepest levels of a well-lived life, but we will find that each one is immeasurably valuable.

Modern culture immerses us in busy lifestyles and continual entertainment, and this has blunted our ability to find meaning in life. Movies distract us, entertainers dazzle us, and flickering screens constantly remove us from considering the things that are most important. Online social networks pacify us, marketing campaigns drive us, and abbreviated text messaging is our common communication tool. All of these fast, confusing, things are trying to move us away from the deeper things of life. Most of us have given up on digging down to the basic, simple treasures of life, and have, instead, chosen to live our lives in a hurried, shallow fashion which gives little time to consider deeper things. There is a better way, and Jesus has come to offer it. It is the way of the Kingdom which is deep and simple.

Each human life, every human experience, is a treasure of eternal value and is significant forever. Our identity is important to God. Our life work is of eternal significance. Every kind word we offer our friends and our children has life-long implications. Even our sexuality is of immense value. Why, then, are there so many voices making the human experience seem so fast, and so shallow? Why, then, is there so much complexity flowing out of Christian culture as well? It's true. Christianity, in our generation, has turned following Jesus into a complex, difficult, mess. In recent days the glossary of terms used in Christian conversations has become even more complex. I hear many people using terms like: kingdom, grace, sonship, community, and justice, and they are being used in so many different ways that I don't always understand their meaning. We would all like to see healthy lives, stronger people, and peaceful families growing as a result of Christianity's influence, but this may not be the case in every modern situation. This may be because Christians seem to be trying to keep up with these "trending" terms without having a simple, childlike trust as they follow Jesus. This lack of simplicity may be making the beautiful adventure of following Christ something difficult—something very tiring.

I must confess, again, that I am partially to blame for this problem. To be specific, it was that complicated, difficult version of Christianity that I lived in for so long—full of striving, and perfectionism, and self-judgment—that has caused Christianity to become repulsive to so many. I once followed Jesus as the King of the Impossible Standard. I demanded that everyone pay honor to that kind of a kingdom. In this way, I helped design and fund many of the convolutions of modern Christianity, and prop up some of the most unattractive conclusions about Jesus. I am very sorry for the way I influenced others in a negative way. I am changing my thinking and my living. I have seen Jesus in a different way, and I am now looking for a totally different kind of Kingdom. Because of the new way I am learning to see Jesus, I am also learning simpler definitions for these same words: kingdom, grace, sonship, community, and justice, and my new understanding is not leading to complexity and soul-fatigue.

Following Jesus into his Kingdom is deep and restful, both when we begin and as we continue with him. Paul wrote, "And now, just as you accepted Christ Jesus as your Lord, you must continue to follow him. Let your roots grow down into him, and let your lives be built on him. Then your faith will grow strong in the truth you were taught, and you will overflow with thankfulness. Don't let anyone capture you with empty philosophies and high-sounding nonsense that come from human thinking and from the spiritual powers of this world, rather than from Christ" (Colossians 2:6–8). Whenever our lives become complicated and confusing, then it might be time to change our direction. When health and peace are not the end results of our spiritual pursuits it might be time to change our pursuits altogether. It is time for each of us to choose to follow Jesus in a simple way. Now, I am not saying that following Jesus is easy. Following Jesus is hard, but not because it is complex. It is the singular, simple focus of Christianity that makes it hard. Choosing to die to selfish, self-directed living, and simply trusting in Jesus is the most difficult exercise of all. Christ compared it to taking up a cross, just like he took one up toward his own death. What makes it restful is that we are never alone, and we are never without the hope of our new, eternal life in God. Christ is always with us, loving us into being.

When Mr. Rogers won a Lifetime Achievement Award in the 1997 Daytime Emmys, he went to the podium, in front of all the stars and important people of Hollywood to accept the award. He held it in his hands and turned to the crowd filling the huge auditorium on national television and gently said, "All of us have special ones who have loved us into being."

I would like to pause here, and point out that an awards show, especially for actors, is not the natural place to consider those who are not present. This event was a celebration of "me" and "mine," for those in attendance, and everyone was either thinking of what they deserved, or what they wanted in terms of accolades from their peers. Mr. Rogers interrupted this self-obsessed crowd and introduced a radically contrary thought. He was going to lead them to abandon shallowness, but it would be, simultaneously, difficult and simple.

After his first comment he made a single request, "Would you just take, along with me, ten seconds to think of the people who have helped you become who you are?"

We must draw a connection from this moment in Mr. Rogers' address to the way that Jesus speaks to each of us. Jesus, when he spent time with his friends, was always talking about how his heavenly Father was so beautiful. He did not offer himself as the object of our attention, but deferred to the one who had influenced him the most. Jesus was helping us to understand how to live into the deepest levels of our treasured human existence by treasuring others. Jesus is always taking us toward the simpler, more eternal things of life. Jesus, as well, never entertained his followers' occasional desire to compare themselves to one another and seek personal accolades. Listen to this painful moment he had correcting his closest friends: "Then his disciples began arguing about which of them was the greatest. But Jesus knew their thoughts, so he brought a little child to his side. Then he said to them, 'Anyone who welcomes a little child like this on my behalf welcomes me, and anyone who welcomes me also welcomes my Father who sent me. Whoever is the least among you is the greatest'" (Luke 9:46–48). Jesus turns each one of us—full of self protection and self promotion—into teachable children when he simply asks us to pause and consider who is really most important to us.

Mr. Rogers, making full assumption that everyone would agree with his request to consider others more important than themselves, softly commanded the whole room with the phrase: "Ten seconds of silence."

There was an awkward moment as the busy, glittery, gigantic auditorium adjusted to being told what to do. There was a sacred change in the atmosphere of the room, when the realization of his sincerity overwhelmed them. He was who he had always been. He was doing what he had always done. He converted confusing, busy, times into little moments of sacred simplicity. The real meaning of careers, lives, works, relationships, and dreams all settled into a single pause of deeper consideration. I propose to you that it was in this moment that we see Mr. Rogers's sacred duty as a Christian minister in full bloom. He was more than a children's educator, he was speaking as an authoritative guide to meaning.

He glanced at his watch, then he said to the audience, "I'll watch the clock."

This is a very short book. I think it may only be ten seconds out of our lives to read the words that follow. All I am going to do is continue to outline the absolute value of simplicity in our lives, and the simple requirements of the Kingdom of God. I think they will be well worth our time.

After ten seconds Fred Rogers said, "May God be with you," and quietly left the stage.

KINGDOM CULTURE

I remember my high school chemistry class. I wanted to mix chemicals and blow stuff up, but, of course, we were not allowed to even touch anything in the lab until we had memorized the Table of Elements. This table outlining the elementary components of the physical universe was on the wall behind the teacher on a huge poster. There were abbreviations and little atomic definitions for every known physical element in the world: oxygen, hydrogen, iron, uranium, and on the list went. We were not allowed to do anything with the compounds, the combinations of these elements, until we memorized them singularly and could fill out the whole Table of Elements by hand. It is the same way with the spiritual elements of the Kingdom of God. We really should not be allowed in the "lab," until we have learned the basics. We need to pause, and refocus on the simplest elements of our walk with God, so that we can mature as believers. We need to be able to name the elementary things of the Kingdom clearly, and be able to put them down on the Kingdom Table of Elements on the desk in front of us.

Higher education, we remind ourselves, does not mean learning totally new ideas that have no relationship to the ideas of the previous years of learning. Higher education simply puts the elementary truths together in ways that will help us solve the more complex problems we may face. I sincerely believe there may be a maturity problem among Christians today because of a failure to understand and memorize the elementary things of following Jesus. The failure to teach the most simple things, and to require everyone who follows Jesus to know and understand them, may have led to the competency problems Christian communities are now facing. All students struggle at the higher levels if they don't have the fundamental things memorized. It is our time to receive the same encouragement, and get a clear, strong grip on the elementary elements of life with God.

There is an amazing passage of Scripture on this very subject. In Hebrews 6:1-3 Paul actually lists the most elementary things of our life with God. He warns us to not try and move past these things to anything more difficult until we have firmly understood and memorized them. This is how the passage reads; I have added my own spacing and emphasis in order to better show the list:

> "So let us stop going over *the basic teachings about Christ* again and again.
>
> Let us go on instead and become mature in our understanding. Surely we don't need to start again with
> the fundamental importance of *repenting from evil deeds*
> and *placing our faith in God.*
> You don't need further *instruction about baptisms,*
> *the laying on of hands,*
> *the resurrection of the dead,*
> *and eternal judgment.*
> And so, God willing, we will move forward to further understanding."

I emphasized several phrases from this passage in order to highlight some of the most elementary things in the Christian life, beginning with "the elementary teachings about Christ." Paul is not, as we have already noted, telling us that we should forget the elementary things when he says we should "move forward to further understanding." No, he is saying these simple things should be learned, first, and firmly built inside of us, so that we can go on to the next things with confidence. These first facts should be memorized well, and they should create no cause for disagreement among us because they are so elementary. We should be able to encourage one another with this kind of direct challenge: "If we don't stand firm on these basic, elementary things, there is no way we can become mature followers of Jesus. Without understanding and believing these elementary things we can never grow spiritually strong."

I remember the first time I studied this passage in college, I did not like it. I was struggling with self-doubt, and was depending on my competitive spirit and my personal accomplishments to make me feel secure in my relationship with God. So, when I read this passage in the New International Version of the Bible, and it said, "let us move beyond the elementary teachings," I wanted to quickly move on to the next passages in the Bible. I did not want to go back and spend any time on the list in Hebrews 6:1-3 because they were, obviously, the passages which only the immature would focus on. I really only glanced at them, and I assumed I already knew them because I had been a Christian for quite some time. I treated this list of elementary things as piddly things to be left behind in my pursuit of the greater things. I was a lot like the disciples who didn't think Jesus had time to love the little children because they were simple as well. I made a mistake! I didn't realize that the simple things that Paul listed in this passage were the very things I so desperately needed to follow Christ in a healthy way! This passage was for both children and grown ups ... and everyone in-between! I have changed my mind about this list of elementary teachings. I am growing in my taste for the fundamentals again, and I really want to dig into these simple things of the Kingdom. I would like to invite everyone to join me and let's dig in to them together. If we choose to submit to them as Kingdom facts, without arguing, and to build them into our lives as the most basic truths of our journey with God, then, just as the Scripture promises, we will all "be taken forward to maturity!"

In every school, in every culture, and in every kingdom there are basic elements that we must learn to trust in order to excel. There are elemental requirements for us in all the places we choose to live and learn. When Jesus began to teach he announced the most important new cultural real estate in the history of all time. He announced the Kingdom of God. It is a real place, and he announced we could go there with him. He also explained that the Kingdom was a way of living available to us now. He said we could learn from it, practice its culture, and enjoy the Kingdom's benefits in this life because he would allow us to connect to it now, not just in the life to come. He taught us to speak to his heavenly Father, and pray "your Kingdom come" on earth as it is in heaven. He taught that Kingdom culture could begin to operate right here on earth, just as it perfectly operates in heaven, if we were to turn our lives toward it. It is an eternal, heavenly Kingdom, and it has eternal, elementary foundations that we can learn right now. We must learn these heavenly basics in order to participate in Kingdom life.

THE BEGINNING

Masonry is the art of working with stones and mortar. It is the essential craft of laying foundations. One of the first things a mason learns is that the first stone, the cornerstone, is the most important. Recently, I read guides on laying foundation stones, and I watched videos on how the pros accomplish the task, because I was working to repair a foundation on a small cottage. I thought I might discover a lot of tips and tricks on mixing mortar, or keeping a perfect line as I went, but what I found was that, in every case, the emphasis was on laying the first stone perfectly. Whether laying a new foundation, or building a simple brick wall, placing the first stone is the most important job! If this first block is level, then all the blocks that come next will be easily leveled. How this first cornerstone is placed, and trusted, will decide the integrity and strength of the rest of the building.

So it is in our journey with God.

To begin a conversation about the elementary things of the Kingdom we must begin with Jesus Christ. Our focal Scripture for this book, Hebrews 6:1-3 begins with "So let us stop going over the basic teachings about Christ again and again." Now, we are going to choose to let our ears hear the positive encouragement in this sentence, instead of taking that challenge as a negative one. This is how we will make it positive: We will not "stop going over the basic teachings" until we have actually learned the basic teachings—the elementary teachings about Christ! This is a sincere challenge for everyone to continue to read this book, and learn how to develop a simple, deep walk with

God. There is a phrase in the amazing poetry of Colossians 1 where Paul outlines the beauty and simplicity of Christ that reads, "So he is first in everything." Jesus is the first element in our walk with God. He is the first teaching in our understanding of the Kingdom. He is the first stone—he is the cornerstone—in our spiritual building. The Psalmist sang, "The stone that the builders rejected has now become the cornerstone" (Psalm 118:22). This building project the Psalmist was seeing was the Kingdom of God, and the first stone—the one on which everything else would depend, everything else would follow, and by which everything else would be measured—would be the cornerstone. Jesus, in our most elementary understanding, is this cornerstone that some have rejected, but we are choosing to receive!

Jesus actually repeated this very same Psalm in Matthew 21:42 when he claimed to be that very cornerstone. Jesus was never uncertain about who he was, and what he had come to do! We now understand that Jesus, himself, is the very first lesson in the Kingdom of Heaven, and without him there are no further lessons. Our eternal privilege is that he will build us together, as his people, to be the place that he dwells! 1 Peter 2:4-5 says, "As you come to him, the living Stone—rejected by humans but chosen by God and precious to him—you also, like living stones, are being built into a spiritual house to be a holy priesthood, offering spiritual sacrifices acceptable to God through Jesus Christ." This is how we understand that the Kingdom of God can only be understood in the context of our absolute trust in Christ as the first, and most important person in the whole universe! This Scripture is also how we know that our relationship with Christ and our relationships with one another are paramount in the Kingdom—we are being invited right into the middle of God's relational, family plan! He is building us all together!

We are interconnected, and we are being built, together, into something eternally amazing. Jesus is the most important part of our relational building! If we level ourselves with his requirements then we can build our lives with clarity and confidence. If we seat ourselves firmly beside him then we will gain the right view of the whole world, and we will see truth as he sees it. By building on Christ as our cornerstone we will be able to build on a perfect anchor, and watch our lives grow in strength and beauty! Peter quotes this very same Scripture about Jesus being the cornerstone in Acts 4:11. He was preaching to the angry, religious leaders who were interrogating him for following Jesus. He continued his announcement that Jesus Christ had been resurrected from the dead and had become the beginning of a new era by proclaiming: "There is salvation in no one else! God has given no other name under heaven by which we must be saved." The Good News of the Kingdom always starts and ends with the exclusive right of Jesus to transport us from the temporary world into the eternal world with God.

Paul sees Jesus, not only as the cornerstone for our lives, personally, but the cornerstone of our entire faith family together. He paints a beautiful picture of us all being built together as a holy place for the Spirit of God to live. Speaking to all peoples everywhere who have given their lives to Christ, regardless of their earthly bloodline or religious cultural origins, he says, "Consequently, you are no longer foreigners and strangers, but fellow citizens with God's people and also members of his household, built on the foundation of the apostles and prophets, with Christ Jesus himself as the chief cornerstone. In him the whole building is joined together and rises to become a holy temple in the Lord. And in him you too are being built together to become a dwelling in which God lives by his Spirit" (Ephesians

2:19-22 NIV). For those of us looking for a home, this is our answer. For those of us looking for eternal purpose, this is it. We can choose to allow God to make his home with us, and we can, then, make our home with him.

Finally, Peter repeats this critical theme again when he says in 1 Peter 2:4, "You are coming to Christ, who is the living cornerstone of God's temple. He was rejected by people, but he was chosen by God for great honor." We notice in these passages that Christ's rejection by the world—especially by the experts who claimed to know everything—is an essential part of the story. We, then, should not expect to receive this same Jesus Christ as the foundation of everything for us, and not expect to receive the same rejection from the world. The Chief Cornerstone has been rejected, and so will those who build their lives exclusively on him be rejected. The "smart," popular majority has always had difficulty receiving Christ as the Chief Cornerstone of life. Even religious people have difficulty with this demand. God spent thousands of years cultivating the hearts of the Jewish people to receive him when he came, and, still, even most of them rejected him. They did not reject Jesus as a good person, or maybe even as a great teacher, but they did not receive him as their Chief Cornerstone. How much more will be the rejection from the world today, when people who know very little about God, who have followed their own selfish ways for centuries, hear us proclaim that Christ is the only way into the Kingdom? This is difficult for many. According to the Scripture, however, there is no other way to build an eternal future without Christ as the First, and Only, and Chief Cornerstone.

Anyone who has ever built a stone wall understands that to try and build on more than one cornerstone would be disastrous. A mason would never put a cornerstone over there, and one over here … and, maybe, one more over there … and then try to build a wall in between them. No matter how hard he tried he would not be able to connect them properly and keep the wall true and strong. There can be only one cornerstone at the beginning of any perfect foundation. This may be elemental, but it also happens to be crushing. Many will struggle with the exclusivity and singular claims of Christ in these modern times. This kind of exclusive claim to Divinity, and exclusive claim for spiritual authority is jeered at around the world. We should expect this from unbelievers, but now it has been entertained in the ears and thoughts of many in Christian culture as well. What I am referring to is the modern Christian's interest in presenting Christ as "one of many" options for finding eternal meaning. The modern message has sometimes become the conflicted proposal of building our lives on multiple cornerstones with Jesus still, somehow, being the Chief Cornerstone. Some have tried to file down and chisel off the exclusive claims of Christ in hopes that no other religion, no other culture, and no other person from any belief system could be offended, but this has only created confusion. Christians have become weak and afraid to stand and repeat these kinds of "Christ is the only way" Scriptures aloud because the reaction and the consequences are so frighteningly obvious. As a result we are suffering in a different way: Not for persecution for preaching Christ, but for leaving the "the basic teachings about Christ" that are challenging us from Hebrews 6.

Jesus knew this challenge would come to us, and was not shy about the problem he was creating. He said of himself, after he referenced being the cornerstone from Psalms 118, "Everyone who stumbles over that stone will be broken to pieces, and it will crush anyone it falls on." If we don't receive him as our singular cornerstone for life, then he will be the stone that crushes our negotiations to death. We can negotiate with Christ's exclusivity as our spiritual foundation using our traditions, our will, or our emotions, but none of these negotiations can be allowed to stand as truth. This is not because he does not love us, but precisely because his love is so perfect toward us. His love lays the foundation for eternal life, and when we build in any other way besides on his perfect love, then we are simply inventing a foundation that will fail. Jesus, according to his own words, is an all or nothing proposal for every person. He loves every one of us the same, but we are faced with a very important decision, and this decision will be contrary to the world's complex and shallow way of thinking. We must choose to stop trusting in our thinking, and start choosing to place our lives squarely, and completely, on Jesus Christ, our Chief Cornerstone.

We have a choice to make right now in our first lesson in the elementary school of Kingdom life. We must choose to confidently agree with the entirety of the Scriptures about Jesus Christ, and agree with over 2,000 years of the Christian faith. If we push back from a full embrace of Jesus, then we will find ourselves in a sea of uncertainty and arguments that never end and lead us nowhere, even if they are popular in many circles. If we continue to negotiate with Jesus, our Chief Cornerstone, then we may start using terms like progressive revelation, spiritual mythology, essence of truth, living documents, and interpretive nuance. These terms have been invented by intellectual negotiators in an attempt to live in their own novel religious philosophies. This kind of "high" thinking only leads to terminal complications. We can't live on the edges of faith when we consider Christ. The truth is a person, not a theological argument. The truth is Jesus. He said in John 14, "I am the way, the truth, and the life." This is a relational proposal: We will receive Jesus as our only cornerstone, or we will reject him.

This is a basic teaching about Christ: Jesus does not save everyone, automatically, because, as some have wanted to say, rather cheaply, God is love. Love has never been cheap, nor has love ever been understood in a context where anything goes. Love is patient and kind, and love certainly forgives, but love also requires great commitment, and always makes the self-sacrificing choice to act on another's behalf. Jesus has acted on our behalf: "But God demonstrates his own love for us in this: While we were still sinners, Christ died for us" (Romans 5:8). God's love is richly poured out toward each of us without any restrictions whatsoever! He has provided every one of us the same rescue, and extended the same loving invitation to join him! Our requirement—and the whole of the New Testament has made it very clear—is that we must choose to place our hope and our lives in his care, and follow him. In other words, we must agree with his love for us! When we agree with him, about everything he has said, and everything his message proclaims then we are "believing in him." Our receiving of Christ and our belief in him—our absolute trust in him—is the action on which our whole journey with God is based. "If you confess with your mouth that Jesus is Lord and believe in your heart that God raised him from the dead, you will be saved. For it is by believing in your heart that you are made right with God, and it is by confessing with your mouth that you are saved" (Romans 10:9–10). Our faith in Christ, alone, is the activation of our forgiveness: "He is the one all the prophets testified about, saying that everyone who believes in him will have their sins forgiven through his name" (Acts 10:43). It is our agreement with God that Jesus Christ is the only way to have eternal life, and to know eternal meaning, that allows us to walk in the truth: "All who believe in the Son of God know in their hearts that this testimony is true. Those who don't believe this are actually calling God a liar because they don't believe what God has testified about his Son. And this is what God has testified: He has given us eternal life, and this life is in his Son. Whoever has the Son has life; whoever does not have God's Son does not have life" (1 John 5:10–12).

Let's remember a few things about Christ that will help us see him as our Chief Cornerstone. He is not called Jesus Teacher even though he did teach. He is called Jesus Christ because he came as a King with a Kingdom. We remember how Jesus spoke of himself when he said, "And just as my Father has granted me a Kingdom, I now grant you the right to eat and drink at my table in my Kingdom" (Luke 22:29–30). This is how we understand that Jesus is the Messiah—the Old Testament word for Christ—which means the one who would come as a King and deliver us into God's Kingdom. Jesus Christ rescues us and leads us out of being captive to the temporary ways of the world, and into his eternal world—the Kingdom of God. Moses leading God's people out of captivity into the Promised Land was a living theater displaying what Jesus Christ would do for each of us who would follow him. He calls us out of our bondages and says, "Follow me," and he leads us into the Promised Land—the Kingdom of God. He also shows us the heart of the Father, as he reaches out to us in love. He recasts our understanding of the heart of our Father when he died for each of us on the cross. If we really saw him, he said, we would also see the love of the Father: "I am the way, the truth, and the life. No one can come to the Father except through me. If you had really known me, you would know who my Father is. From now on, you do know him and have seen him" (John 14:6b–7)! This is amazing to consider that the King who rules the Kingdom of Heaven would want to intimately engage each of us in a loving, close relationship. This tells us about our King, and it tells us much about the nature of his Kingdom.

Jesus referred to himself as the I Am, just as God announced himself to Moses in the burning bush:"'I tell you the truth, before Abraham was even born, I AM!' At that point they picked up stones to throw at him. But Jesus was hidden from them and left the Temple" (John 8:58–59). When he uses this name for himself, I AM, there were many who would not believe this claim because it was so clearly and intensely Divine. His very name, Immanuel, means God With Us (Matthew 1:21), and this name belongs only to Jesus. He is the King of Kings and Lord of All (Revelation 19:16), and this is a position which has no equal. There is no other God, and there is only one God of three distinct persons who loves us all together: the Father, the Son, and the Holy Spirit (Matthew 28:19). The Trinity is inseparably in love with one another, and eternally in love with us. Jesus Christ was God who came to us, personally, to express his love.

The disciples were never confused about who Jesus was; they knew he was God. Paul says, "Now to the King eternal, immortal, invisible, the only God, be honor and glory for ever and ever. Amen" (1 Timothy 1:17). Jesus, to make his Divinity clear, claimed to have absolute authority in every realm. Jesus said of himself, "All authority in heaven and on earth has been given to me" (Matthew 28:18). He also said, "All things have been committed to me by my Father. No one knows who the Son is except the Father, and no one knows who the Father is except the Son and those to whom the Son chooses to reveal him" (Luke 10:22). This transfer of absolute authority to Christ is an eternally significant moment. He said, all things, not some things, had been committed to him. This is why we see Jesus Christ as the inauguration of a new era in God's plan. This is the era where the Kingdom has been transferred to Christ, and he, in turn, invites us to be a part of it with him! The reason the Kingdom was given to Jesus was because he submitted himself to Father God. The reason Jesus shares the Kingdom with us is because we submit ourselves to him! Philippians 2:8-11 says that because "he humbled himself in obedience to God," that "God elevated him to the place of highest honor and gave him the name above all other names, that at the name of Jesus every knee should bow, in heaven and on earth and under the earth, and every tongue confess that Jesus Christ is Lord, to the glory of God the Father."

In the Kingdom, we discover, that authority and honor flow from submission and obedience. Jesus is our perfect example of submission and obedience. He submitted to the Father's heart because he knew it was always good, and obeyed him even to the point of dying a criminal's death on the cross so we could be restored to a relationship with God! God is committed to a healthy relationship with us, because he is, as God, a perfect relationship—he is the Trinity of love. Jesus shares with us the ability to know the Father, personally, as a gift: "When I am raised to life again, you will know that I am in my Father, and you are in me, and I am in you. Those who accept my commandments and obey them are the ones who love me. And because they love me, my Father will love them. And I will love them and reveal myself to each of them" (John 14:20–21). It is Jesus's deep desire that we would be able to see, and know, and love God in a real, and eternal way. Eternal life—which is a healthy relationship with God—is given to us as a gift: "My sheep listen to my voice; I know them, and they follow me. I give them eternal life, and they will never perish. No one can snatch them away from me, for my

Father has given them to me, and he is more powerful than anyone else. No one can snatch them from the Father's hand. The Father and I are one" (John 10:27–30).

These things I have quickly summarized about Jesus are the very essence of the Gospel. They are some of the simplest things of our faith in Jesus Christ, and some of our most "basic teachings" about him. They help us understand what it means to receive him as our Chief Cornerstone. I didn't reference every Scripture that support the statements I just made, but it will take very little effort to read the Bible and easily discover them. They are plain and obvious, they are repeated often, and these basic truths require no special ability to understand them. The question we must begin to ask now, is, "Will we believe them?"

Our challenge is to say aloud, "Jesus Christ is my answer for everything!" Jesus can never be our partial answer for anything because God, himself, isn't able to be tacked on to a collection of anyone's best ideas. We can do that with gurus, teachers, prophets, doctrines, and religions, but we cannot do it with Jesus Christ, our heavenly King. Let's pray aloud and make our choice clear!

I believe in Christ, and I don't want to add anything or anyone else to him! He is complete and perfect in all things, and he is first in everything for me.

I have placed my trust in Christ, alone, and I do not trust in my good works or anything else to make me right before God. He is my goodness, and he has made me good through his gift of love!

I have asked Jesus to forgive me of my sins, and my broken relationship with God. I trust Jesus alone to forgive me, and to restore me to a right relationship, an eternal relationship, with God.

Jesus Christ is the Chief Cornerstone of my life. He is the joy of my life! I will worship him! I will depend on him! I love him!

I will announce that Christ is my truth, my way, and my life! I will receive the Kingdom of God as my destination and my heavenly source. I will share my faith in Christ just like Paul shared his:

"If you confess with your mouth that Jesus is Lord and believe in your heart that God raised him from the dead, you will be saved. For it is by believing in your heart that you are made right with God, and it is by confessing with your mouth that you are saved. As the Scriptures tell us, "Anyone who trusts in him will never be disgraced." Jew and Gentile are the same in this respect. They have the same Lord, who gives generously to all who call on him. For "Everyone who calls on the name of the LORD will be saved."

But how can they call on him to save them unless they believe in him? And how can they believe in him if they have never heard about him? And how can they hear about him unless someone tells them? And how will anyone go and tell them without being sent? That is why the Scriptures say, "How beautiful are the feet of messengers who bring good news!"

But not everyone welcomes the Good News, for Isaiah the prophet said, "LORD, who has believed our message?" So faith comes from hearing, that is, hearing the Good News about Christ. But I ask, have the people of Israel actually heard the message? Yes, they have:

"The message has gone throughout the earth,
and the words to all the world." (Romans 10:8–18)

When Paul is confronted with those who wanted to make some adjustments to the simple message of Christ, and Christ alone, he uses some very hard language: "Let God's curse fall on anyone, including us or even an angel from heaven, who preaches a different kind of Good News than the one we preached to you. I say again what we have said before: If anyone preaches any other Good News than the one you welcomed, let that person be cursed" (Galatians 1:8–9). He should be cursed not only because the false preacher is twisting a sacred message from heaven, but because Paul knew that adding other foundations to the Gospel would bring people into a weak and destructive life. We care for one another's best future and so we have to challenge one another to a single, strong foundation! There is no way around it. We have to make a choice. Either Jesus Christ is our one and only Chief Cornerstone, the first and most important part of our spiritual foundation, by whom everything else in all of life in heaven and on earth is measured, with no negotiation, no replacements, and no options, or … he is not. If he is our Chief Cornerstone then we are like the wise man in the parable who builds his house on a rock and when the storms come the house stands firm. If we try to have more than one foundation then the many parts will become like the many parts of sand. They will shift, move, and be unpredictable. Our house will crumble and fail because our foundation was not single, not sure, and not built on Christ alone.

This first, elementary teaching from Hebrews 6 may seem a little tough when we first confront it, but I am reminded that it is with great love that Jesus came to us, and with great love the disciples have taught us how to think and live in agreement with God. My heart is like Paul's heart when he shared his love with the Christians in Ephesus: "When I think of all this, I fall to my knees and pray to the Father, the Creator of everything in heaven and on earth. I pray that from his glorious, unlimited resources he will empower you with inner strength through his Spirit. Then Christ will make his home in your hearts as you trust in him. Your roots will grow down into God's love and keep you strong. And may you have the power to understand, as all God's people should, how wide, how long, how high, and how deep his love is. May you experience the love of Christ, though it is too great to understand fully. Then you will be made complete with all the fullness of life and power that comes from God" (Ephesians 3:14–19).

THE SOURCE

The elementary foundations of our life with God are smooth and in simple shapes. These next two building blocks of Kingdom life fit together like A and B, and they fit perfectly alongside the Chief Cornerstone, Jesus, in our understanding. As we move forward in this book, I would like to assume that we have decided to trust Jesus as our Chief Cornerstone. So, as believers, together, let's go on and discover all of these amazing foundational teachings! The basic teaching about Christ in Hebrews 6:1-3 makes possible the next two foundational teachings, in this order: *repenting from evil deeds* and *placing our faith in God.*

Learning how we are to repent from evil deeds is like learning to read a map. A map is a drawing that shows us not only where things are in the world, but more importantly where we are in it! We begin to read a map properly by assessing our personal starting point. We first find the "you are here" symbol on a map to know our position. In Hebrews 6 we are told to repent, or to turn away, from evil deeds. Some translations say, "repentance from acts that lead to death," or "repentance from dead works." In any Scripture reading we see that not all actions lead to life; some actions lead to death and are useless to us. We should discover what these acts that lead to death are, and make an immediate commitment to turn away from them! In order to turn away from anything we must first know where we are, and in which direction we are headed. This is kind of like understanding our spiritual GPS coordinates as we consider our walk with Christ.

As we place a finger on our spiritual map we try and understand where we are, and where we are going. Many people try to get to heaven by starting from here (as they place their finger down low on the map where they think they are), and working toward there (as they draw their finger up to a higher place on the map toward God). So many of us who love Jesus have continued to try and make our path to heaven from where we are now, to where we think he is. We say, "Well, I am not who I used to be," and so we draw a dot on the map of our life, the beginning of our journey, and we try to draw a line toward heaven. We say, "Well, I am thankful I am not like them anymore," as we reference those further below us on our map, and this allows us to trace our finger along the line we draw toward heaven and confirm that it seems to be going in the right direction. We long for heaven, and so we sing about it, we write poetry about it, and teach our children to go to Church and be good. We hope that in good time, with these good efforts, we will somehow make it to our heavenly destination.

This, however, is wrong thinking and has nothing to do with following Jesus.

Here is the fact the Scripture teaches us, and that Jesus worked so hard to make clear to us all: you can't get there from here.

This kind of thinking that says we can work from where we are to where God is, is a deeply flawed understanding of our spiritual GPS and of the true map of our lives. We have to recalculate our coordinates. Jesus took a moment to explain this in John 3 to Nicodemus who was also trying to get there from here. Nicodemus saw Jesus as a man from here, so he called him a teacher, but Nicodemus also thought Jesus was a man who knew about there, because his miracles seemed to be from heaven. Jesus answered him by saying, in affect, "Dear Nicodemus, no one can even see the things of the heavenly realm unless they are born there." He said, "I tell you the truth, unless you are born again, you cannot see the Kingdom of God" (John 3:3b).

This is how we understand being born again. We were born first in this world by an earthly mother. We began in blood and tears and love, but we began right here in this world. Everything that is born in this world dies in this world. What originates from here doesn't have any right or ability to take flight into the next world, even if it had wings of great teaching, great upbringing, and great intentions. Jesus told Nicodemus that no one could enter the Kingdom of God, the eternal life with God, unless he was born again in a spiritual way. Being born again would allow each of us to wake up through tears of joy, just like at a natural birth, but rather than being covered in the elements of this world, we would be covered with the heavenly world, filled with the Spirit of God, and alive with Christ in a whole new place! We could be born again into a new heavenly family, and immediately find ourselves seeing what we could have never seen on our earthly maps! When our spiritual rebirth happens we wake up in the realm of the eternal Kingdom! Jesus changes our starting point. He changes our spiritual GPS coordinates in a miracle of rebirth. He changes it from here to there.

Take out a clean sheet of paper and draw a horizontal line right across the middle of the page. Now write Kingdom of Heaven at the top, and the kingdom of this world at the bottom. Draw a dot somewhere in the bottom half and a line from it pointing toward the Kingdom of Heaven ... but, wait ... you can't cross the line you drew that separates the two halves of the page. "For everyone has sinned; we all fall short of God's glorious standard" (Romans 3:23).

Say aloud, "I can't get there from here."

Now, draw a new dot above the line in the Kingdom of Heaven and write your name beside it. Aha! When we give our lives to Christ, this is our new location after our rebirth into the Kingdom! When we are born again we start here—in the Kingdom of God. Now draw a line toward the Kingdom of Heaven. Well, now, that was easy because we are already there. Our efforts toward Kingdom life once we are born again in Christ, are to simply practice being who we really are! Jesus transforms us internally, and he transports us into a new position with God—we only have to agree with what he has done and who we are in the heart of God. The line we draw toward the heavenly Kingdom after our rebirth in Christ is a totally different kind of trajectory, because it no longer tries to cross anything that separates us from God. Our trajectory is already in God, and we simply put into practice the enjoyment of our new life with him! Our new life does not reach to what it can't attain, it aims at what has been given to us through Christ. In this new picture we don't strive to work toward heaven, rather, all our striving is to simply agree that we really are heavenly citizens. We work to agree with God about our new nature—our new life—in Christ!

This is how we understand that our source for life, and our destination in life are both in Christ. This is how we correctly understand our Kingdom GPS coordinates. This is also how we understand how to turn away from dead works. Hebrews 6 plainly points out that we are to repent from "dead works." What this means is, as believers, we can, obviously, still participate in the actions, the mindset, and the forces at work below the line on the page marked the kingdom of this world. Everything below the line is dead works because it is not sourced and destined in the eternal Kingdom of Heaven. We can, amazingly, have our new

GPS "you are here" dot relocated into the heavenly realm, but we can still, unfortunately, choose to live our lives from an earthly position. That is to say, we can still live as though our spiritual GPS is stuck in the earthly realm, and choose to use the things on this earth, the powers it holds, and the stuff it promises as our source for living. How tragic! This should not be! This is a dead way to live, and it is a choice we must stop making. We must choose to live from our new Kingdom position and repent from dead works!

Yes, there really are earthly elements that build a worldly culture. We say worldly because the source and destination of this culture is in this earthly, temporary, world. The world has a specific set of ways, styles, philosophies, and practices, etc., that builds its culture. But, once we choose to follow Christ then our source and our destination have completely changed, and so has the culture in which we are to live! This world is passing away, so these are not the things we will choose to live by. Peter refers to the failing strength of this world like this: "But the day of the Lord will come as unexpectedly as a thief. Then the heavens will pass away with a terrible noise, and the very elements themselves will disappear in fire, and the earth and everything on it will be found to deserve judgment. Since everything around us is going to be destroyed like this, what holy and godly lives you should live, looking forward to the day of God and hurrying it along. On that day, he will set the heavens on fire, and the elements will melt away in the flames. But we are looking forward to the new heavens and new earth he has promised, a world filled with God's righteousness" (2 Peter 3:10-13). Peter used the word elements like we would use them in the Table of Elements from chemistry class, but his point was that the Table of Worldly Elements is going to disintegrate and melt away. These kinds of worldly elements often come to us disguised as heavenly truths, but they leave us striving for the next revelation, or the next insight, or the next secret that will make us strong and mature. These worldly ideas offer themselves as spiritual truth, but they do not satisfy like the truths from the eternal realm. This is why Jesus spoke of the deeper satisfactions of Kingdom truths when he said to the woman at the well in Samaria, "Everyone who drinks this water will be thirsty again, but whoever drinks the water I give them will never thirst. Indeed, the water I give them will become in them a spring of water welling up to eternal life" (John 4:13b–14). Jesus was talking about worldly elements when he referred to "this water". The things that come from this world, including both the physical and spiritual realm, are not going to satisfy us for very long.

Remember, when we use the word elemental we are not just speaking about the physical components of the earth, like on a Table of Elements from chemistry class, but we are also speaking of the elemental spiritual forces of this world. These are the spiritual thoughts, spiritual powers, and spiritual teachings that are sourced from this earth, but do not have an eternal destiny. These "elements" do not lead us into the eternal culture of the Kingdom, but, instead, they build a temporary culture that begins and ends on this earth. Just as heavenly beings and heavenly teachings can influence our lives, these worldly spiritual beings and worldly teachings can also influence our lives. We should learn to identify them, and turn away from them! Paul warns of them in Colossians 2:8, "See to it that no one takes you captive through hollow and deceptive philosophy, which depends on human tradition and the elemental spiritual forces of this world rather than on Christ" (NIV). Apparently, these "elemental spiritual forces of this world" lead a person to obsess over eating and drinking, rules and regulations, and to lean toward the supernatural powers that can be touched and used in this world. These forces entice us to focus on the mystical, consult the spirits, and engage the powers that exist here with us—whether for healing or harming—but these things are all destined to perish. Paul goes on to warn, "Since you died with Christ to the elemental spiritual forces of this world, why, as though you still belonged to the world, do you submit to its rules: "Do not handle! Do not taste! Do not touch!"? These rules, which have to do with things that are all destined to perish with use, are based on merely human commands and teachings. Such regulations indeed have an appearance of wisdom…" (Colossians 2:20-23, NIV). These worldly teachings appear wise to us because they are popular. Today, popularity has become synonymous with wisdom. But these earthly spiritual forces, even if they are popular, are no longer useful for us as followers of Christ. Why? It is because they belong to a temporary world, but we belong to an eternal world! They appear wise because they mimic the heavenly realm, but they are not wise at all because their source and their destination is not from the Kingdom of Heaven. Their source and destination is still from this world.

Paul went on to explain that if we continue to try and draw our journey to heaven from where we stand on the earth that we would end up in endless competitions, comparisons, and problems. This way of thinking, to him, was immature and would lead us to think and act like slaves, instead of like sons in the Father's Kingdom: "So also, when we were underage, we were in slavery under the elemental spiritual forces of the world. But when the set time had fully come, God sent his Son, born of a woman, born under the law, to redeem those under the law, that we might receive adoption to sonship" (Galatians 4:3-5, NIV).

The only way out of orphaned wandering is to be miraculously transferred into the Kingdom, as sons, by adoption. We can't think our way to heaven. We can't work our way to heaven. It is only the miracle of Jesus' love that has made our heavenly rebirth possible. We will enter his Kingdom by trusting Jesus, and we will continue to enjoy his Kingdom with the same childlike trust.

Now, we can also say that the Kingdom of God is built on elementary things. These things are different from the elementary things of this world. The elementary things of the Kingdom are from a different source altogether. They are not derived from, nor are they discovered in, this world. We have to be born again in a spiritual way, according to Jesus, before we can even see them! This means that only Christ can reveal to us what is appropriate for us as Kingdom citizens so we can live in Kingdom culture. Now, Jesus Christ, we have learned, is both our source and our destination. When we live in this way the Bible calls it "living by the Spirit." Romans 8:9 illustrates our new life in the Spirit this way: "But you are not controlled by your sinful nature. You are controlled by the Spirit if you have the Spirit of God living in you" (Romans 8:9), and then goes on to explain that the Spirit only comes when we trust in Christ. When we walk in the Spirit, we are saying that we are walking in harmony—in agreement— with the Spirit of the Kingdom of Heaven. Living by the Spirit, then, does not mean to just have a mystical connection with the impressions and revelations we may receive from God, no, it means that we live our whole lives in agreement with the ways of the Kingdom—the elemental ways of God's own culture. This may include the leadership we receive in very spiritual ways, but walking by the Spirit is a much broader proposal. It is the opposite of living according to the world's ways.

Living by the Spirit is the opposite of living in dead works. Romans 14 explains that the Holy Spirit will teach us to live in agreement with God, and this is how we learn to live by the Spirit. This is a simple way of living, but it may take some time to become sensitive to the Holy Spirit's leadership. Not every young believer is perfect at knowing the difference between the heavenly source and the earthly source, but we can all learn this over time if we become students of the Holy Spirit's influence. The process of learning to identify God's leadership is a maturing in spiritual discernment. There are four legs on the Table of Discernment. The Table of the Discernment is where we learn to differentiate between what is right and what is wrong, from what is heavenly and what is worldly. One leg is the Holy Spirit, the Presence of God in us, who leads us into truth. However, we are learning to hear the voice of God a bit at a time—and this is a challenge for all of us—and so we have more than a one-legged table. We also have the Scriptures. God's word builds in us an understanding of how his loving heart works, what he has already taught us, and how we are to live. Learning to study and understand God's word takes some time, too, so we don't have a two-legged table, either. We also have the Christian tradition. Yes, Christians have been helping one another to follow God for 2,000 years and their collective understanding is very important to consult. The common practice, liturgy, teaching, and rhythms of the Christian tradition are tried and true. Sure, there have been some mistakes along the way, but by and large, our Christian history must be given a chance to speak into our Christian present. Our learning from Christian history is definitely not complete, and so we do not have just a three-legged table. The fourth leg on the Table of Discernment is the present family of God, the Church. The Church is the people of God that love us, and are in our lives to help us and be our comrades in real time. We know that God places people in our lives to help us, to pastor us, and to challenge us, and, so, we receive their influence as vital and sacred as we learn the ways of the Kingdom together. These four legs will make our Table of Discernment strong and stable when they are in agreement with one another. We can, with the agreement of all four legs, learn how to confidently turn away from dead works, and participate in heavenly works. We should be wary of those who lean on only one leg and ignore all the others.

When these four things weave together we have a better understanding of what it means to live by the Spirit as Paul encourages in 1 Corinthians 3:1. This is a holistic view of living. Living by the Spirit, as we can see in many Scriptures, involves our minds, our spiritual gifts, our wills, our communities of faith, our heritage, and our maturity to practice what we have learned. We no longer live by external laws of rightness, or by internal feelings of rightness, rather, we live according to the way of the Kingdom which is, first, to follow Christ in the way he has shown us. He teaches us about Kingdom living through many different things, but the outcome is that our lives are changed from the ground up, and that Jesus is always lifted up and honored by everything we do. Living, then, by the Spirit will always be evidenced by how our lives lift up Jesus, and bring peace to the family of God. Living in the Spirit will always bring those who walk by the Spirit into closer fellowship, and it will not tear us apart. According to 1 John this is how we can know who is born of the Spirit and who is born of the flesh. John says it this way, "So we are lying if we say we have fellowship with God but go on living in spiritual darkness; we are not practicing the truth. But if we are living in the light, as God is in the light, then we have fellowship with each other, and the blood of Jesus, his Son, cleanses us from all sin" (1 John 1:6-7). Living by the Spirit always builds up the family of God.

The command to turn away from worldly source and worldly practice is so intense around this elementary lesson in the Kingdom that we are told not to even associate with believers who continue to engage in worldly things. Paul says, "When I wrote to you before, I told you not to associate with people who indulge in sexual sin. But I wasn't talking about unbelievers who indulge in sexual sin, or are greedy, or cheat people, or worship idols. You would have to leave this world to avoid people like that. I meant that you are not to associate with anyone who claims to be a believer yet indulges in sexual sin, or is greedy, or worships idols, or is abusive, or is a drunkard, or cheats people. Don't even eat with such people" (1 Corinthians 5:9–11). Why is this warning so strong? Because the health of God's family is paramount! The lesson, in practice, is that we will always end up playing the game the people we are with are playing. It's like practicing baseball. If all our friends play baseball we will learn the game and practice it, but if all our friends play another game then we are likely to learn that game and play along as well. This has nothing to do with unbelievers, but it has everything to do with our fellowship with one another as Christians. This is why fellowship and close camaraderie with other healthy believers is an essential part of a healthy, maturing spiritual life. We must learn to practice the same things together—the ways of the Kingdom—in order to grow healthy as God's family.

Practicing is doing something you know how to do.

Trying is performing an action you don't know how to do.

We are not told to try righteousness, we are told to practice it. We know how to live in the world, and from the world, because we have been practicing that our whole lives, but now that we are in Christ we can't practice that any more. Now that we have been transported into the approval of God by our rebirth in the Spirit we can no longer try to live with God—we simply practice living with God. John says, "Those who have been born into God's family do not make a practice of sinning, because God's life is in them. So they can't keep on sinning, because they are children of God" (1 John 3:9). That's right, it is an impossibility for those who have been born of God to continue practicing earthly thinking and earthly works, because we have been changed from the inside out and transported into the heavenly realms! If we do worldly things anyway, we will find out that they only lead to confusion, complexity, and destruction. We are to practice heavenly works because everything from the Kingdom of God will stand forever! Righteousness—deep, simple, rightness before God—is a gift from Jesus, and it is alive in us by the power of the Holy Spirit. Paul says, "And because you belong to him, the power of the life-giving Spirit has freed you from the power of sin that leads to death"(Romans 8:2). So much of Romans 8 paints a beautiful picture of our new righteousness that has been given to us by God. Christ's message was not about what we should do in order to conquer the world and become righteous, but how to let the Kingdom of Heaven conquer us with its righteousness. He does not lead us to escape the world, rather, he leads us to become citizens of a brand new world. He announced that he was our only passage to heaven, and he proclaimed that all of our trying to get to eternity by obeying laws and rules was at an end. Paul says, "Brothers, listen! We are here to proclaim that through this man Jesus there is forgiveness for your sins. Everyone who believes in him is declared right with God—something the law of Moses could never do" (Acts 13:38–39). He was putting an end to trying to be good, he would share his infinite goodness with us!

So, we have clearly seen, that we can be Kingdom citizens, even while still in earthly bodies living on this planet, but we still must choose which citizenship we will live by—which one we will practice. This, again, is what it means for us to "turn away from dead works." This is how we understand the encouragement: "So then, just as you received Christ Jesus as Lord, continue to live your lives in him," from Colossians 2:6. This affirms that we don't live from the earth toward the heavens. We live from the heavens into the earth. What I mean to say is that our rebirth changed our starting point, therefore, we do not return to our old starting point and to try to "live for Jesus." Now, we start from a heavenly point, and we continue to live in Jesus, not for him. When we continue to live our lives in him then we are living from a heavenly source, but we are living it out in this world—we are living from heaven to earth! The age of striving and working is over. The age of trying to get there from here has come to an end. Jesus has made a way, the only way, to enter heaven and it is through himself. This is why Paul says so eloquently, "God saved you by his grace when you believed. And you can't take credit for this; it is a gift from God. Salvation is not a reward for the good things we have done, so none of us can boast about it. For we are God's masterpiece. He has created us anew in Christ Jesus, so we can do the good things he planned for us long ago" (Ephesians 2:8-10). We now have a heavenly perspective just like Paul said, "For he raised us from the dead along with Christ and seated us with him in the heavenly realms because we are united with Christ Jesus" (Ephesians 2:6).

Let's expand our understanding a little more. On the bottom half of the page you have been drawing the two Kingdoms—the Kingdom of Heaven, and the kingdom of this world—write the words: healing, prophecy, miracles, praise, submission, and justice on the lower half. These things can be sourced and manifested in and from the kingdom of this world. These things are not necessarily from heaven, because there are powers in the temporal realm that seem to accomplish all of these "good works". The spiritual realm in this world is active all the time, it is inhabited by powerful spiritual beings, and is constantly seeking to influence and engage with us. Just because these spiritual powers look heavenly does not mean they are. Jesus tells a story about those, at the end of the age, who say to him, "Lord, Lord, didn't we do all these things in your name…" Yes, in that illustration the people did many good looking things, but they did them in the world, and from the world. Jesus said, "On judgment day many will say to me, 'Lord! Lord! We prophesied in your name and cast out demons in your name and performed many miracles in your name.' But I will reply, 'I never knew you. Get away from me, you who break God's laws'" (Matthew 7:22–23). From the sorcerers in Egypt to the charlatans of the New Age people have continued to do supernatural and heavenly looking works foolishly quoting things like "a kingdom divided against itself cannot stand." They quote this Scripture passage from Luke 11:17 in order to try and prove that everything that looks good must come from heaven, but they fail to read the rest of the passage where the power that comes from the eternal realm always preaches the Kingdom of God, and brings order, and beauty, and cohesion to Christ's family. It is foolish, then, to say of anything that looks good that it is a "Kingdom thing." Neither can we say of unbelievers: "They are doing Kingdom things," when they do things that appear to be good things, any more than we could say of the sorcerers of Egypt who made sticks into snakes: "They are doing Godly miracles." We must choose to say, "It is not whether it looks like a good thing, it depends on its source and its destination being in the Kingdom of God."

Remember, Jesus has offered us no chance to self-design strategies for doing eternal works. These self-designed plans only result in earthly, dead works. He has offered only one source for our daily needs and it is to depend on him, alone. He has given us the power we need to live as Kingdom citizens both now, and in the life to come, and we can choose to receive that power to live in the Kingdom exclusively in Christ, or we can continue to struggle looking for power and secret insights from this world. If we don't receive Christ as our only source of power, then we will probably consult horoscopes, be entertained by mediums, look into energy fields and metaphysics, seek special knowledge, and spend our money on the latest discoveries and the most novel treatments for our problems. We will also look into things less spiritual sounding—but full of the promises from this world, nonetheless, like: shiny things, money, houses, cars, fortune, and fame on the stage of life. We might even aspire to things we consider noble like: family, justice, benevolence, healing, and honor. For many of us that have a more religious orientation, we will find ourselves adding ceremonies, prophecies, memberships, revelations, or covenants to the simple journey of trusting in Christ, alone. These extra things will present themselves to us as essential to our faith, but they are misrepresenting themselves. They will present themselves as the preeminent treasures in life, or at least present themselves as treasures on par with Christ. This is a dark competition among things that want to find a seat of equality beside Christ. We must refuse their advances, and be ready to worship only one essential treasure—Jesus Christ—and have everything else fall in line behind him! There is only one Cornerstone, and he, alone, is essential! Christ is our ultimate treasure above all things, and we must build our lives on him if we are to find eternal meaning. We will eventually find that all of these other competing powers—all of these complex, fast moving solutions—are all driven by the false promises of this temporary world. All of these essentials are, really, just distractions. They are all false sources, and only lead to death because they are not sourced from Christ, alone.

Now, take your pen and draw a line from the Kingdom of Heaven part of the page you have been drawing on down across the center dividing line to encircle each of these words: healing, prophecy, miracles, praise, submission and justice … you just made them all eternal works! You connected their source to the Kingdom of Heaven, and now they have eternal benefit! It's just that simple. I am not trying to say that God will bless whatever we do when we draw an imaginary line to it; no, what I am saying is that when our lives and works are truly sourced from God they are eternal, and when they are sourced from the earth they are dead works. When we operate from our trust in God, with our source in him, then everything we do is an eternal work. These works stay on our account—they are our "treasures in heaven" that Jesus taught us about!

God knows our hearts in these things, and it would be wise for each of us to take a deep look into our hearts and test our motives and activities to see if they originate from God. We must grow very sensitive and stay away from earthly-sourced spiritual insights, and the voices of influence that we are not absolutely sure are from God. We understand that the four legs on the Table of Discernment must all be employed together to give us a confidence as we choose right from wrong. When we take the time to allow all four legs: the Holy Spirit, the Scriptures, Christian tradition, and our present Church family to influence our understanding, then we will be able to make wise choices to live in an eternal way. We will practice the things that are clear in Scripture, and not practice anything in the gray areas. We will practice trusting God, but we will not practice homosexuality or any unhealthy sexual lifestyles. We will practice helping others, but we will not practice manipulating others—even for great causes. We will practice an awareness of the eternal realm, but we will not practice supernatural experiments on each other. We will practice obeying the word of God, but we will not practice doing good things just to impress other people. We will practice praying for those that are sick, in Jesus name, but we will not put our trust in special oils or incantations. We will stay away from the mission of enacting justice in this world from a worldly perspective which is full of emotion and revenge, because we choose to sit at the feet of Jesus and receive his justice and his judgment in all things which is sure to come. Why can we say these things so clearly? We are just outlining very simple things we have learned as we have placed them on the Table of Discernment. We are learning to put our trust in Christ alone, and see that nothing has eternal value unless it comes from him, and he directs us in it. We are choosing to agree with the Kingdom way, and live by the Spirit in everything we do. Now that we understand what dead works really are, we are choosing to turn away from an earth-sourced life, and focus on finding our foundation in Christ, and our source in the heavenly realm at all times! Some people belong to this world and can't understand these things at all. They only see from where they stand. "Those people belong to this world, so they speak from the world's viewpoint, and the world listens to them" (1 John 4:5). People with a worldly mindset will always seek to justify their earthly attitudes with heavenly sounding sentiments, but they do not have the ability to even see the Kingdom, much less understand it. But we, who have found our lives completely built on the Chief Cornerstone, Jesus Christ, have been transported into heavenly realms, and now live every moment of our lives for eternal significance, and eternal meaning, and we have turned away, one-hundred-and-eighty degrees away, from dead works that are sourced from this world!

TRUSTING GOD'S HEART

Did you know that in Sir Arthur Conan Doyle's books that Sherlock Holmes never actually exclaimed, "Elementary, my Dear Watson!"? That phrase actually came later in the film versions of the story and became popular because it summarized a lesson Sherlock was often trying to teach his friend. He was fond of proving that the solutions to most mysteries were in the unnoticed details. It was the small things, the overlooked things, that often provided the clues to solving the mystery that was in front of him.

In the mystery *A Scandal in Bohemia* Sherlock challenged Watson's ability to keep up with him in the art of noticing and absorbing the simple facts. He asked him how many times he had come up and down the steps to his flat on Baker Street.

Watson replied, hundreds of times.

Then Sherlock asked him, how many steps are there?

Watson had no answer, to which Sherlock replied, "Quite so! You have not observed. And yet you have seen."

Many of us have walked up and down the stairs of our own spiritual journey, but we have not observed each one in a way that we could confidently name them as individually important. This, however, is the essence of following Jesus and living a healthy life. We must be aware of the important things in his Kingdom—the simple treasures of our walk with him—and pause to consider each one by name. Sherlock announced to Watson, confidently, that there were seventeen steps. He knew because he had looked at them with the intent of knowing them, and he committed them to memory on purpose. Seventeen steps up to the flat on Baker Street may have seemed trivial at first, but in a Sherlock Holmes mystery we learn that everything can be important, especially the simple things.

In a Sherlock Holmes mystery novel the key to solving the unknown is always in noticing the small things and coming to a conclusion—a deduction—based on the simplest of facts. Sherlock would notice a spot of dirt, a ruffled collar, or a single missing book from a shelf and in these simple details he was able to come to the truth and solve the mystery. He did not discover the truth through complex philosophies, and he often blamed other investigators' apparent blindness on their tendency to get wrapped up in fast-thinking and complex ideas.

This should be a rich encouragement to us all. This life is, indeed, full of mysteries. Sometimes understanding the message of the Bible seems mysterious when we first enter the conversation and we are not sure what to focus on. Paul even said in 1 Timothy 3:9, as he was defining how to recognize trustworthy men: "They must be committed to the mystery of the faith now revealed and must live with a clear conscience." There was a time when people had no idea what God was really up to, but now, through Christ, his plans have been revealed! He was making a way for us to be close to him, to know him, and to enjoy his Presence forever!

Following Christ is not complicated. However, when the practice of our spiritual lives gets distracted from the simplicity of following Christ, then it will become complex and confusing. There are all kinds of voices, noises, proposals, and facts swirling all around us, all vying for our attention. They can make our lives complicated. Jesus steps right into the middle of this confusion and says, "Follow me." He offers a simple solution. He shows us that simplicity really is the key to walking in the Kingdom way. The decision to follow Jesus will be taken one simple step at time, just like the steps up to the flat on 221B Baker Street.

One of our first steps is "placing our faith in God," just as it reads in Hebrews 6:1-3. Faith involves three simple things. It involves learning that God is always good, that God is always acting in love toward us, and that our trust in him will always be tested. First, let's ask ourselves if we really believe that God is always good. How could we, after all, place our trust in a God whose heart was in question? This might be a clue to answering why we are prone to lean on our own thoughts and our own efforts so quickly, instead of trusting God, alone. The question of God's goodness is found in the first few pages of the Bible. It is found in the Garden, at the very beginning of our story:

"Did God really say…?" the serpent asked Eve.

The enemy of our faith asks the same questions of us today: "Did God really say?"

We all understand this question is aimed at the goodness of God's heart. It was meant to turn a simple choice of trust in the Garden of Eden into an accusation against God's good heart. While the enemy was still talking we can imagine Eve, agreeing in her own mind, "Be quiet, snake, I can't think. I am trying to figure out what the trick is … God's love must be too good to be true!" The possibility that God's heart is too good to be true has caused each of us mental problems—just like Adam and Eve. The mysteries of life come, and though we can hear God saying, "I love you, you can trust me with everything…" the serpent's deception is planted in our hearts, and we have found ourselves agreeing with him:

God might be not telling me everything.

He could be holding something back.

Maybe God loves others, but not me.

Maybe I need to look in another direction for help …

And then it all falls apart.

The serpent said of the fruit on the Tree of the Knowledge of Good and Evil, "God knows that your eyes will be opened as soon as you eat it, and you will be like God, knowing both good and evil" (Genesis 3:5). The enemy of our faith didn't make the Garden, and he didn't make the Two Trees of Choice. The enemy had no trust equity with anyone, but he has all of us questioning the goodness of God's heart. In his very next breath, he sold Adam and Even the lie that he had special knowledge, some hidden insights, that would make them feel whole and safe. He has told each one of us that we would be better off inventing our own way to right living.

Remember, the opposite of faith is not believing there is no God, it is not knowing if we can trust the God we believe in. When we are not sure of God's heart, then we usually change the object of our faith to an earthly source. Our key passage from Hebrews 6 says, specifically, that our simple, elementary lesson is to place "our faith in God," and this is the very opposite of putting our trust in this world—or practicing dead works! The enemy asked us to do just that! He asks us to eat from the knowledge and judgment found in this world, and to derive our sense of rightness from our own insights. This is the opposite of trusting in God. If the devil wins and our fears overtake us then we will turn toward earthly answers for our problems because all of his deceptions lead us back down to the temporal, earthly levels. Most believers won't be caught failing their tests of faith by standing up on a desk and shouting, "I don't believe in God anymore!" No, most will fail by turning their gaze down away from heaven and looking in their desk drawer for something familiar, something "practical" they can use to make it through without having to depend totally on God. But can earthly powers, and earthly things, solve eternal problems? Can the things within our control, and under our command, solve the things that are out of our control? No, we must put our faith in God.

We remember that the message of the Kingdom is called the Gospel, the Good News of the Kingdom. Jesus has done something for us that is so good it is beyond our definition of good! Jesus shows us in a perfect way that God is always good, always good to us, and always good for us. It is God, himself, from whom every perfect gift flows down to us (James 1:17). He can be perfectly trusted because he loves us so perfectly. If we are tired, we must remember that God is with us, and that he is helping us in every way! Listen, Paul says, "For God is working in you, giving you the desire and the power to do what pleases him" (Philippians 2:13). Once again we see that God's loving heart deserves the credit for everything! We must never fear that he will come through for us. We are reminded again from the passage in Ephesians 3:18-19a, "And may you have the power to understand, as all God's people should, how wide, how long, how high, and how deep his love is. May you experience the love of Christ, though it is too great to understand fully!" Jesus, through his self-sacrificing love, even to death on the cross, is showing us the ever-trustworthy heart of God. Jesus said when we see him, we would see the Father as well. When I see Jesus dying for me, I know that God's heart is always good, because even when I didn't care, he still reached out and died for me.

This leads us to consider the second thing we said about faith: we must know that God's heart is always toward us in love. It is not enough to believe that he is good—we must believe that he is good for us! If he remains uninvolved with us, or uncommitted to our well-being, then we would have reason to believe that his heart was not good, and that we could not trust him. We must think clearly and ask ourselves this question:

Does God do tricks, or does God do miracles?

The answer to that question all depends on what we believe is the purpose of God's heart. A trick, defined, is when something from an earthly place, dazzles our eyes and does something amazing in front of us. We are amazed, but later we find out it was not real. The intent was not true toward us. Tricks are designed to conceal something. They are a flash—a sleight of hand—to distract us while we are deceived into believing something that is not true. We pay people on earth to do tricks for us. No one, however, wants to be tricked by God.

A miracle, to be clear, is when the Divine invades our world and does something wonderful for us. It is a supernatural act of love, and it is given to us to show us that God really loves us. It is what we hope for in God, and it is what we cry out for when we are in trouble. No one has ever prayed for God to do a trick on their behalf when they were in trouble. We all pray for miracles. When no answer can come from the earth we look to heaven for a miracle, and we do this even if we don't consider ourselves religious in any way. Why? Because it adds depth and beauty to our lives if we can really believe in a God who loves us! We all want to know if we really needed a rescue that God would come through for us. We need to believe that he would do so, not because he has to, and not because we could manipulate him, but because he genuinely, eternally, loves us. Here is the great news! God will, even before we ask him to, act in love toward us. Romans 5:8 says, "But God showed his great love for us by sending Christ to die for us while we were still sinners." The Psalmist sang, "They cried out to you and were saved. They trusted in you and were never disgraced" (Psalms 22:5). This word disgraced is like the word shamed. When we trust in God we will never be shamed. It is not his desire to shame us, and he will never trick us.

When we needed God most he performed the best miracle of all! Into the middle of our troubled, thistle infested Garden he appears and he reaches down to the ground and pulls up the things that have wounded us. He weaves a crown of thorns out of these broken things, and wears them on his head. He has no trouble doing for us what we could never do for ourselves. He has shown us that only an invasion of love from an eternal world can ever conquer the troubles we have gotten ourselves into.

Jesus is our miracle.

Now, we have a choice to make as we engage the mystery. We will have to choose to trust God's heart because we believe that his heart is always, always good for us, and that he is always acting in love toward us—without exception. We call this kind of life or death trust: faith. As the Scriptures say, "It is through faith that a righteous person has life" (Romans 1:17). We can't have faith in someone we don't believe is good, and God is proving his goodness every time we hear more of the story of Jesus! We also know, "it is impossible to please God without faith" (Hebrews 11:6), and therefore, it brings God no pleasure if we continue to live from our own logic, our own plans, and our own power. This is the reason I have spent so much time on the intent of God's heart, because without believing that God is good, in every way and at all times, it is impossible to have faith.

We have to choose to trust Jesus to forgive all our sins. We trust that he makes us right before God, because he loves us so much. We must choose to believe that God has done it from heaven, not using worldly tools and efforts, because his heart is love. When we make our confession that this is our truth, that Christ, himself, is our righteousness—no longer our human effort—then we are saved from the temporary world and all its deception. This is faith. And it is based on the loving heart of God, not on our efforts. Faith is not the same as trying, though many use the word like this today. They say, "Tell me about your faith," when they mean to say, "Tell me about how you try to please God." They say, "She has great faith," when what they often mean is, "She tries really hard in her religious practice." This is not the faith we are required to have in Hebrews 6. Our faith is a simple and deep trust that God's heart is always good toward us.

Now, let's also remember that trust must be tested so we know it is authentic. Our faith must be proven to be valuable. Untested faith, in other words, is just wishful thinking—and that is not how we follow Christ. We will have continuous choices in our lives to either trust God, or look to the world for our help. We are going to have many opportunities to answer the snake's question, "Did God really say?" When we hear this question it will be our time to say, "Yes, we did hear him, and we trust him in every way!" This is the way believers are to always live: "So then, just as you received Christ Jesus as Lord, continue to live your lives in him, rooted and built up in him, strengthened in the faith as you were taught … " (Col 2:6–7).

We should not be surprised that in the story of our beginnings with God in the book of Genesis that our trust was immediately tested. We test the trust in our own children often, and early. We say, "Son, enjoy playing in the back yard just don't play in the mud and ruin your pants." We also announce on the same day, "Daughter, enjoy the swimming pool just don't run on the pool deck or you'll get hurt." Now those commands may not sound like tests, but they are. Each command is simply a test to see if our children have learned to trust us and stay safe in our watch care. Never once did we think we would be accused of setting our children up for failure by trapping them in an evil and tricky challenge! That is ridiculous! We were expressing our love in a world of good and bad choices, and we expected our children to obey—not because it fulfilled us, but because each test was preparing them for adulthood. Yet, within fifteen minutes Johnny came in the house covered in stinky mud, and Sally had two skinned knees and a bloody lip from falling on the pool deck.

To have faith in God we have to trust him, and we have to pass some trust tests so we can grow strong and mature. Little children learn to trust their parents a little bit at a time, and often through countless repetitions of failing the same test over and over again. The Bible begins our human story with us failing a faith test, covered in mud and bleeding from the lip. The Two Trees in the Garden represented a healthy choice of trust, and an unhealthy choice of mistrust, and we failed the test. But God did not give up on us. God set in motion a plan to train us out of our juvenile delinquency, and into maturing adults. He set in motion a plan to help us learn how to trust him, and he worked on this plan for thousands of years. It always involved learning to trust him, and his laws for right living were supposed to move us in that direction. When he gave the Law to Moses in ten basic rules for living, he was showing the people the way of heaven, but it did not show them the way to heaven. This gap was supposed to increase their need to trust him, but instead they wanted to trust in their ability to keep the Law in their own power. And we think our kids are hard to raise?

Again, a tested faith, is not a trick from God. It is his way of helping us build a solid, love relationship with him! God wants to have an ongoing, loving relationship with us so he allows us to make a choice to trust him. Here is a question to make the point: Have you ever been successfully forced into loving someone? Sounds ugly does it not? There is no way to make that sentence become lovely. Try it. Say it aloud:

I was forced into loving that person.

Sounds criminal, really. The answer to people's assertion that the Bible begins with a fantastically sadistic trap in the Garden of Eden is so easy to answer that children understand it. Even children know that love involves choice because as soon as being forced enters the sentence we know that love has made its exit. When we give our own children directions that involve choosing a safe path and avoiding consequences like mud and pain, we are not setting them up for failure, we are preparing their lives for greatness!

When we put our faith in God we can join with Abraham who, "Never wavered in believing God's promise. In fact, his faith grew stronger, and in this he brought glory to God. He was fully convinced that God is able to do whatever he promises. And because of Abraham's faith, God counted him as righteous. And when God counted him as righteous, it wasn't just for Abraham's benefit. It was recorded for our benefit, too, assuring us that God will also count us as righteous if we believe in him, the one who raised Jesus our Lord from the dead" (Romans 4:20–24). Abraham may have never wavered in his faith, but he did make some mistakes. Abraham's faith was tested in order to strengthen his heart of trust, not to prove him perfect in every action. Faith has to be tested so we can prove that something exists between ourselves and God. Most of our faith challenges will come when we have to hang on to what God said even when nothing in this world seems to be proving it is coming true. We have to believe that God is taking us to higher places and trust him, regardless of the circumstances. We don't put our trust in the outcomes that we can measure, we are putting our trust in God's heart that we have proclaimed to be good toward us, always. That is why the classic definition of faith in Hebrews 11 says, "Faith is the confidence that what we hope for will actually happen; it gives us assurance about things we cannot see."

Whether we grew up in a religious home, or we were born in an anti-Christian culture, we are on the same journey once we put our faith in Christ. When we put our faith in God, he will prove himself to us. Remember, James does not say, "If," he says, "When troubles come your way, consider it an opportunity for great joy. For you know that when your faith is tested, your endurance has a chance to grow" (James 1:2–3). Peter doesn't say that we should avoid our tests of faith, he says we should, "Be truly glad. There is wonderful joy ahead, even though you have to endure many trials for a little while. These trials will show that your faith is genuine. It is being tested as fire tests and purifies gold—though your faith is far more precious than mere gold" (1 Peter 1:6–7a). Our opportunity to choose God, and God alone, creates in us a love that grows, and a faith that takes on a substantial strength. In this world our life is filled with broken things and beautiful things. It's a mess. It is filled with pain and success, joy and failure, beginnings and endings. It is unpredictable. It is not in these temporary, fading, crazy things that we will find our source or our solution. No, it's in the eternal goodness of God toward us. That is what makes our faith so strong! We are learning that God's heart is always good, and when we have our trust tested it gives our faith literal substance! Faith is not just hoping for what we want, faith is believing in who God really is, and how he really loves us.

So, then, faith is learning that God is always good, that God is always acting in love toward us, and that our trust in him will always be tested. In order to dig into this mystery of truth, and grow strong in it, we will have to develop our taste for the ways of God. We will have to learn to recognize his leadership and his Kingdom order. We must learn to understand when something is from him, as a gift from heaven, or when it is a good looking thing that is actually sourced from this world. "Dear friends, do not believe everyone who claims to speak by the Spirit. You must test them to see if the spirit they have comes from God. For there are many false prophets in the world" (1 John 4:1). Part of the testing of our faith is to learn the loving, trustworthy voice of God. We must learn to recognize the sound of heaven. Here are some more practical clues for discovering the sound of heaven. These are questions that help us discover if something from God:

When did it originate?

Where did it come from?

Who did it come from?

What does it lead to?

When we ask *when it originated* we are looking for its connection to Christ's announcement of the Kingdom of Heaven. We are looking to test every voice of influence by its literal connection to the narrative of the Scriptures. If it was introduced when Jesus proclaimed the arrival of the Kingdom, if it is clear in Scripture as being part of the Kingdom, then we have a clue to the trustworthiness of the source.

When we ask *where it came from* we are looking into the literal geographical place as well as the philosophical place of the voice. If it comes from a culture of faith in Jesus Christ then we have a clue that the source is heavenly, but if comes from an unbelieving philosophy or a doubting mindset then we can be suspicious. If it comes from a culture and a place that has no hold on following Christ, then we should be very, very careful before we place our trust in it.

When we ask *who it came from* then we are looking into the lineage of the source. We are looking at the family tree of the voice of influence. In the Bible everything was connected through family lineage, and in the Kingdom everything is connected the same way. It is right and healthy to allow our trusted spiritual family to introduce us to Kingdom sources, and it is right and healthy to mistrust a source that is delivered outside the connections of the family of faith. We are speaking broadly here, not just to our local small group, but to the Christian family as a whole.

When we ask *what it leads to*, we are checking on the destination of the voice and its influence. If it is promoting Christ alone, and in agreement with the Kingdom way that begins and ends with Jesus, then it is a clue toward its value as a Kingdom source. It if it is trying to "get there from here," using earthly thinking and tools, then we have an obligation to turn away.

These four questions can help us learn to hear God's voice more clearly so we can place our faith in him. They are not perfect questions, but if they are all taken together, they can be very helpful to us. We could consider adding these kinds of wise questions to our understanding of the Table of Discernment. God has given us a rich set of tools, and if we weave them altogether we will grow in our confidence in hearing and obeying God.

The enemy would be happy, very happy, if we would stoop to finding our source in things from this world because then our mindset would be earthly and we would never look to the eternal source that we have been given in him. We would always be tired, and always be running out of energy for life. Every difficulty would send us looking for a new answer, a new book, and new remedy for our heart's aches and pains. The deceiver would be tickled if we would continue to try find the solution for our difficulties in this life, from tools we find in this world, especially the interesting ones, because it would keep us from seeing the eternal tools that God has already provided for healthy living. The enemy would like to have us locked into weak, childish lifestyles, and he can do it if he can convince us to put our faith in anything, but God. When we place our faith in God alone, however, we can expect to grow strong and healthy in this life, and to expect a heavenly reward! "It is impossible to please God without faith. Anyone who wants to come to him must believe that God exists and that he rewards those who sincerely seek him" (Hebrews 11:6). I desire his heavenly rewards. My prayers for everyone, in this moment of challenge to trust God, alone, is that we would overcome our fears of being vulnerable. Sometimes trusting the things we can see in this world is so much easier because there is no relational component. When we talk about trusting God, however, the subject becomes extremely relational, and all our fears about trusting others come to the surface. I pray for our courage to lift our arms to heaven and to allow our heavenly Father to pick us up, and to take care of us just as he has always longed to do. Our decision to trust him will allow us to discover a God who can transform the word vulnerability into something beautiful.

TRUSTING GOD'S WORD

Drink your milk.

When I was a little boy my mom would say, "Son, drink your milk. It will help you grow up big and strong!" The dairy industry apparently was in partnership with my mother because they followed up with commercials that said, "Milk! It does a body good," and they printed billboards that read, "Milk is good food!" Milk is full of basic nutrients that babies need to start growing and keep growing, and even as we get older we continue to dunk our cookies in it, and pour it on our cereal. Because of the joy of ice cream, we never seem to outgrow it!

Milk, in the story of our journey with God, represents the nourishment to become strong and healthy. God said, in the story of Moses and the escape from Egypt, "So I have come down to rescue them from the power of the Egyptians and lead them out of Egypt into their own fertile and spacious land. It is a land flowing with milk and honey..." (Exodus 3:8). Paul is speaking to the Corinthian believers about living in their spiritual strength instead of their earthly weakness when he says, "Dear brothers and sisters, when I was with you I couldn't talk to you as I would to spiritual people. I had to talk as though you belonged to this world or as though you were infants in the Christian life. I had to feed you with milk, not with solid food, because you weren't ready for anything stronger. And you still aren't ready, for you are still controlled by your sinful nature" (1 Corinthians 3:1-3a). It is time that we expect one another to grow up and mature in our spiritual lives. I heard a man say, "You can always grow up, but immaturity can last a lifetime." This struck me as true, because I have heard people use mature sounding Christian words, but have watched them remain weak and frail in their spiritual lives. This should not be the case with us. We should not just get older, we should become more mature!

Paul continues speaking to any of us who want to become spiritually strong. He simply says to us, "You must drink your heavenly milk!" We need to drink the teachings from the Kingdom of God so that we will grow up as healthy adults in our spiritual life. If we turn to the food from this world to nourish our souls, we will find that we will become weak and frail. The problem we all face is that we have already learned to "eat" from what this world speaks to us. Its speaks words like competition, self-protection, and judgment, and all these words make us weak. God wants us to eat from his words because he will make us strong! Paul expands his thoughts on our spiritual diet like this, "Anyone who lives on milk, being still an infant, is not acquainted with the teaching about righteousness. But solid food is for the mature, who by constant use have trained themselves to distinguish good from evil" (Hebrews 5:13-14, NIV). Growing up means, quite clearly, being able to understand what is right and what is wrong. So receiving the milk of God's word is the process of learning to agree with God at all times, not just to memorize passages of Scripture that we never put into practice. These "teachings about righteousness" are the beautiful ways of God, as well as how to put these ways into practice. This is the Kingdom way, and it is clear in the Kingdom what is right and what is wrong. The simple, good news is that God teaches us right from wrong if we are willing to drink in the simple milk he has for us in his Word! In Peter's first letter he also writes, "Like newborn babies, crave pure spiritual milk, so that by it you may grow up in your salvation, now that you have tasted that the Lord is good" (1 Peter 2:2-3, NIV). The elementary things of the Kingdom of God taste good, and if we nurture our deep affections for his words then we will become strong!

In Hebrews 5:11-12 Paul couches a similar encouragement in a warning. He says, "In fact, though by this time you ought to be teachers, you need someone to teach you the elementary truths of God's word all over again. You need milk, not solid food!" This passage immediately precedes our key passage from Hebrews 6:1-3, and it sets the stage for the purpose of this book. Paul is reminding us that if we try to eat grown up food before we have established a healthy diet of milk then we will be in trouble. If we don't believe the simplest things from God, there is no way we can handle the more difficult things of life. Even though we may try to move on to more mature spiritual subjects, if we are weak in our diet of the basic words God has spoken we will not be able to excel. Drinking the pure, simple, basic nutrients of God's word helps us understand how to know right from wrong and become adults in the ways of the Kingdom.

Now, when God wants to say something he often uses words. This is why God spoke to Adam in the Garden, and he wrote on tablets of stone for Moses, and he gave the prophets lots and lots of things to say about his intentions in the world. He was using words. Because he is God I believe he was always choosing his words wisely. When God wants to say something really important like, "I love you," he is even more careful with his words.

Some things shouldn't be said in a letter.

Some things shouldn't be said even by a messenger.

Some things need to be said in person.

John 3:16 says it so succinctly, "For God so loved the world, that he gave his one and only son…" and when God sent him to us it was the perfect moment of communication. Father God, in his great love for us, had spoken the perfect word to say, "I love you!" The Gospel of John begins with, "In the beginning was the Word," and this was, of course, Jesus. Then, just a few sentences later, he makes it very specific: "For the law was given through Moses, but God's unfailing love and faithfulness came through Jesus Christ" (John 1:17). Jesus really is a love word! Jesus, as our Chief Cornerstone, is also the first and the final Word as God relays himself and his purposes to us!

Though Jesus is the perfect Word of communication with us, we also know that God uses even more words to communicate his heart to us. Listen to what Paul thanks the believers in Thessalonica for: "Therefore, we never stop thanking God that when you received his message from us, you didn't think of our words as mere human ideas. You accepted what we said as the very word of God—which, of course, it is. And this word continues to work in you who believe" (1 Thessalonians 2:13). Paul referred to his own spoken words as the "very word of God." He was not speaking of them like a bronzed collection of religious writings—we don't even have these exact words he is referring to written down in the Scripture, but he was referring to his confidence that he was speaking in agreement with God. The proof of his words being from God was how they were continuing to "work" in those believers' lives to build their trust in Christ. The disciples' teachings and leadership, and subsequently their writings, were considered so trustworthy that much of what they said eventually made it into the Bible. In the same way we trust Paul's words were from God. Someone could come to me today and simply say, "Ben, it is time for you to trust Christ with your life," and, sure, that, too, would be God's word for me. We say that because we are confident that God's heart was clearly in the encouragement. This is the same way we refer to the Bible being God's Word, but the Bible has the added confidence of millions of great believers, over thousands of years, proving that what was written down does, indeed, contain God's heart for us!

Even during the life of the apostles they were already referring to one another's letters as Scripture. Peter writes, "So then, dear friends, since you are looking forward to this, make every effort to be found spotless, blameless and at peace with him. Bear in mind that our Lord's patience means salvation, just as our dear brother Paul also wrote you with the wisdom that God gave him. He writes the same way in all his letters, speaking in them of these matters. His letters contain some things that are hard to understand, which ignorant and unstable people distort, as they do the other Scriptures, to their own destruction" (I Peter 3:14-16). That's right, Peter referred to Paul's letters in concert with the "other" Scriptures. He meant Paul's letters were already, in his view, a part of the whole collection of Scripture. We are learning, then, that God uses many different kinds of words to lead us into the Kingdom. We trust first in the Word who is Christ, and then we also trust the great people who have walked with Jesus who speak the truth to us. This is encouraged when Paul says, "Remember your leaders who taught you the word of God. Think of all the good that has come from their lives, and follow the example of their faith" (Hebrews 13:7). The milk of God's word comes to us by trustworthy people, and it comes to us in the simplest teachings in the Scripture.

These days we have a distinct advantage over the first century believers, in this regard: the words collected in the Scripture—the whole Bible—have been proven to us as beautiful and trustworthy as the very words of God! It is important for us to understand that receiving the Bible as God's Word has been clearly established over millennia. How Paul's letters, or James' writings, for instance, made it into the Bible is important, but in every case it was because the greater believing community recognized the voice of God in these writings, they had proven over time to be very useful, and key leaders met together over many, many years to agree on which books, letters, and content would be collected as the Word of God. We have already seen that some of what the apostles said was already considered God's Word before any meetings discussing their teachings had even been held. But after countless years and a great many believers agreed together that their teaching was, indeed, God's word, then the collection we call the Bible was formed.

This is a very important moment in learning how to place our faith in God. I have added this chapter as a way to further intensify the elementary teaching in Hebrews 6 to trust God without exception. This is the point I would like to make clear: If we believe God sent his perfect Word, Jesus, to share his heart with us, don't we think it is time we begin to believe that he chooses all his words with perfect wisdom? The Bible is God's Word. God spoke only one perfect Word, but he has spoken many words in the Bible that help us learn, grow, heal, and mature in Kingdom life. The Bible is not our messiah, nor is it the fourth member of the Trinity. It is sad that many traditions have tried to make it so. What it is, however, is an indispensable tool in discovering God. Paul tells Timothy, "All Scripture is God-breathed and is useful for teaching, rebuking, correcting and training in righteousness, so that the servant of God may be thoroughly equipped for every good work" (2 Timothy 3:16–17).

The Bible we have today is the Bible we need. To think otherwise is to have no faith in God that he could choose his words wisely. Why have we entertained so many questions about the trustworthiness of Scriptures, their sources, the translations, etc., if it is not the serpent deceiving us with the same question, "Did God really say?" Yes, God really did say, and we believe that such great care has been taken by God to preserve what he said so we could all trust it in its written form today.

Paul believed that all Scripture was God-breathed. This is an amazing statement, and one that must be added to support this simple spiritual lesson: trust God's word. Paul was a scholar in understanding the collections of the Old Testament books of the Law, the Prophets, and the Writings. Jesus referred to all three of these sections when he says, "'When I was with you before, I told you that everything written about me in the law of Moses and the prophets and in the Psalms [part of the Writings] must be fulfilled.' Then he opened their minds to understand the Scriptures" (Luke 24:44–45). He didn't say that some of the things written about him would be fulfilled, but that everything in the Old Testament collection that pointed to him would be fulfilled! Just like the people that Jesus was teaching, we don't need a better Bible—we need Jesus to open our minds to understand what we have!

So many Christians these days are afraid of the Old Testament. It's as though once the "letters in red" show up in their Bibles they would be content to just erase the earlier part with all its chaos, delinquency, laws and requirements. But Jesus says in Matthew 5:17-19, "Don't misunderstand why I have come. I did not come to abolish the law of Moses or the writings of the prophets. No, I came to accomplish their purpose. I tell you the truth, until heaven and earth disappear, not even the smallest detail of God's law will disappear until its purpose is achieved. So if you ignore the least commandment and teach others to do the same, you will be called the least in the Kingdom of Heaven. But anyone who obeys God's laws and teaches them will be called great in the Kingdom of Heaven." When Jesus referred to the Scriptures in this account he was referring to the Old Testament. In Luke 24, even after Jesus had been resurrected from the dead and was miraculously visiting with the disciples, he focused on explaining the Old Testament to them. This is what he did when he appeared to them on the Road to Emmaus. Most of us would have liked him to fly around or shoot flame out of his hands to prove he was God! No! He explained to them the Scriptures about himself! Why? Because this is elementary to our trust in God. We trust him, and we trust in his word. We believe that God chooses his words wisely.

The whole Bible, then, is useful, and critical, for our spiritual strength and maturity. Both the Old and the New Testament are full of trustworthy words from God. They are absolutely necessary for us to even know how to approach God. It is also necessary for us to give an explanation of our faith in God. In Acts 8:26-40 Philip is sharing the Gospel with a stranger from Ethiopia. The story literally starts with an angelic visitation, it continues with the Holy Spirit speaking to Philip, and ends with him being miraculously, literally, transported to another place. What helped that key leader from Ethiopia find faith in Christ was not the dynamic miracle, or the angelic visitation. Philip explaining the Scriptures to him is what led him to faith in God. When the Ethiopian heard the message in the Scripture explained to him, he decided to put his faith in Christ alone. He was immediately baptized into the family of faith. In 1 Peter 3:15 we are challenged, "if someone asks about your Christian hope, always be ready to explain it." It is elementary for us to expect every believer trusts the Scriptures, and can explain them to others. Paul instructs the young leader in 2 Timothy 3:14, "But as for you, continue in what you have learned and have become convinced of, because you know those from whom you learned it, and how from infancy you have known the holy Scriptures, which are able to make you wise for salvation through faith in Christ Jesus." The Bible is the sure place where we learn about God's love, and how we learn about the way of the Kingdom of God.

Though our modern Bibles took many years to develop, collect, and be translated I believe every step of the way was overseen by the Holy Spirit and that what we have really is God's trustworthy word, and I believe it is very powerful. According to its own claims: God's word heals us (Proverbs 3:1-8), and it illuminates our minds (Psalm 119:105). It prospers us (Psalms 1:1-3), and helps us overcome sin (Psalms 119:11). It cleanses us (Ephesians 5:26), and it is bread for living (Luke 4:4). It corrects us, and it helps us mature (2 Timothy 3:15-16). All these things about God's words have been proven to be true by those who have tested them. It is true, I laugh every time I see a television news program running a commercial on how trustworthy their news program really is. Shouldn't an objective third party be deciding that? Well, when the Scripture makes claims about itself, it is allowing countless proofs and millions of changed people all over history to give an objective score to its authority. The Bible has been proven to be trustworthy in all respects by both scholars, and normal everyday people just like us over cultures and countries for centuries.

It is important to build the trustworthiness of the Scriptures into our first lessons in Kingdom life because we live in a culture where secular independence and human logic has permeated everything around us. The Bible, in stark opposition to worldly thinking, sets itself as an unmoving standard from God, a word that works like a measuring device to divide right from wrong, and it makes no room for subjectivism and change on the fundamentals. It relays to us the eternal standard. Because of this conflict with the course of humankind the Bible was the first thing to come under attack as dated and untrustworthy during the Enlightenment of the 17th Century where men begin to think of themselves as the centers of the universe. This "enlightenment" toward earthly-thinking came to us through the advancements of science and industry, and it soon trickled into our philosophical and social understanding as well. The Bible continued to be attacked and diminished in all the philosophical and leadership schools that came from that era, including Christian academics. These "high minded" thoughts have become common thinking in our times. The influence of earthly-minded men has been adopted by popular culture with statements and catch-phrases that include:

The Bible is a living document, therefore it, and we, must grow up together.

These ancient Bible stories can't be brought forward to have meaning in our modern world because they were meant for another time.

Understanding the mythologies of the Bible stories is subject to each one's opinion and cultural bias. We must discover the truth behind the words, not the truth of the words.

God does not judge people with discriminatory laws like the Old Testament seems to relay—he couldn't because he is love, and judgment is hateful.

There is a progressive revelation of God's purpose and he is not done showing us all he wants to show us about his plan for humanity. We should remain open to new revelation and new voices of authority in knowing God's plan.

The Bible was written by man in his own image, and men can't be trusted. The Bible, really, is just an elaborate collection of stories that powerful religious men use to control the rest of the world.

All of these statements seem to accomplish only one thing: they try to erode our trust in God's heart for us. They are designed to have us question his uncompromising goodness and unbendable power to do what he says. They are designed to have us question his unwavering commitment to choose his words wisely. We must make a stand. We must affirm, first, that God is good. Then we must affirm that he is always loving toward us. Then we must be confident that he will test our faith with the troubles and trials in this world. All that being said we must also trust in the Scripture as God's Word for us. We must believe he is capable of communicating well with us. The words God has spoken into our Scriptures can be trusted from top to bottom, without question because we trust God communicates with clarity. We must stop measuring his word by popular sentiment and how we feel about it today. It has already withstood the scrutiny of millions of lives changed. This is part of placing our faith in God.

When we visit the Louvre in France to see some of the most classic works of art in all of history, we do not go there to critique the art. We go there to allow the art to critique us. It has already been proven to be great, we are looking on them in order to adjust our understanding of greatness. To open our mouths and question their greatness is simply to diminish ourselves because they have been so thoroughly tested and proven to be great works of art. When we humble ourselves and allow our tastes to be influenced by these great works of art, then we will grow in our appreciation and fondness for beauty. As we learn how to appreciate them, we learn new words to adore them and to honor them as great works. So it is with the Bible. We do not read and study to critique it. We read the Bible so it can critique us. Its greatness is irrefutable. The art of God's love language is unmatched. It has proven the test of time, and it has been proven as more trustworthy, more tested, and more powerfully applicable to the human question than any other literary work in all of history. Now, as we submit to its greatness, we are being transformed by it. We are learning to appreciate it, and to be fond of its beauty in whole new ways. We are no longer trying to conquer the Bible, we are allowing the Bible—as God's word—to conquer us.

IMMERSION

Ask any kid in elementary school how to solve basic math problems and he will say, in the simplest of terms, the matter-of-fact way to do it. First, they would say you need to know your numbers. Ask any kid in elementary school how we learn to spell words, and he would explain to you that, first, you must know your ABC's. Yes, we need to know our 123's and our ABC's in order to pass elementary school. We put them together to form simple words, and solve problems like one plus one equals two. At this level there really is very little room for negotiation. It is just basic stuff, and each one of us has to take these facts, at face value, as true. This is also why the Christian faith is not based on feelings, but in learning to trust in the simplest facts we learn in following Jesus. We work to put the basic elements in place—like our ABC's and 123's—so that later on, in the higher grades, higher learning can take place. No one matures in understanding if they can't first grasp the basics.

Math is the way of understanding how numbers work together. We could also say that the elements of any culture create a certain kind of math—cultural math. My friend, Tim, was in a math class where he was having trouble solving a certain page of equations. He showed his teacher his work, expecting to get reprimanded for being unable to solve the problems, and to his surprise his teacher encouraged him with these words: "Tim, you understand the math just fine, your trouble is with the calculations!" When Tim tells the story he mimics his teacher's thick Irish accent which lends the story more weight. The Irish are known as insightful story-tellers, and, so, here is the insight from this quick story: we don't need to judge ourselves as failures because we sometimes have trouble understanding every high-level calculation of spiritual truth in our lives. God does not judge us according to how perfectly we understand every issue around us. As human beings our ability to understand everything is very limited. God, however, is committed to teaching us the basic math of the Kingdom because it is the way things really work together for eternity. He knows that, eventually, we will learn how to solve the most difficult problems in our lives as we get better and better at his basic math. As we learn the cultural math of the Kingdom the meaning of life actually gets deeper and more simple every day. God is very patient with us, just like Tim's math teacher was with him.

Passing through water is a significant part of the math of the Old Testament. The whole Bible is a narrative of God's pursuing love for us. In the Old Testament we find some of the most dramatic, and clear presentations of how the Kingdom of Heaven really works. The first major journey through water was the story of Noah where the few that survived God's judgment had to pass through 40 days and nights of a flooded earth. When it was all over Noah and his family started a new life, and God was with them.

The second passing through water would have been Israel's miraculous escape from the bondage in Egypt through the waters of the Red Sea in which their captors were drowned to death. The waters parted and they walked right through from a life of enslavement to a whole new life of following God.

Another word in the Bible used to speak of passing through water is baptism. Noah went through a baptism into a new life.

Moses went through a baptism into a new life. And now we, by following Christ, can also go through baptism into a new life!

In these two Old Testament examples of baptism we can draw some very basic understanding about our baptism into our new lives in Christ. Baptism is an immersion in something, and a passing from one thing to another. When we are baptized we are surrounded with something that is all encompassing, and then our passage through it marks a change from one life to another. The old life can't come with us after baptism. In effect, it is dying to the old way, passing through a transition, and entering a brand new life. Both of these clear examples of baptism in the Old Testament brought about a new life with God, and an invitation to follow him in a new way.

Baptism in the New Testament follows the same steps that Noah and Moses experienced. Peter says of Noah's baptism: "Only eight people were saved from drowning in that terrible flood. And that water is a picture of baptism, which now saves you, not by removing dirt from your body, but as a response to God from a clean conscience. It is effective because of the resurrection of Jesus Christ" (1 Peter 3:20–21). Peter underlines what we have already seen about baptism, and he ties together the process of dying to our old life—which we can't go back to anymore—and our new life that comes through Christ. Paul enforces this simple teaching on baptism when he says to us, "Have you forgotten that when we were joined with Christ Jesus in baptism, we joined him in his death? For we died and were buried with Christ by baptism. And just as Christ was raised from the dead by the glorious power of the Father, now we also may live new lives" (Romans 6:3–4). Baptism is the public announcement of our partnership in the death, burial and resurrection with Christ Jesus, and our new life in God.

Remember, the basic building blocks of our faith are all closely connected. Baptism encourages us to leave behind the dead works of our previous life and take hold of our new life which comes from Christ! It symbolizes our passage from the worldly realm, to the eternal realm of the Kingdom. It is now our privilege to place our faith in God. Our faith in God asks us to follow God wherever he might lead us. Concerning Moses' baptism, Paul writes, "I don't want you to forget, dear brothers and sisters, about our ancestors in the wilderness long ago. All of them were guided by a cloud that moved ahead of them, and all of them walked through the sea on dry ground. In the cloud and in the sea, all of them were baptized as followers of Moses. All of them ate the same spiritual food, and all of them drank the same spiritual water. For they drank from the spiritual rock that traveled with them, and that rock was Christ" (1 Corinthians 10:1–4). Isn't this amazing? In this note, as well, we see that our new life in Christ is from a heavenly source, not an earthly source! The story of the Exodus, and the life of Moses, both exist to point us to our journey with Jesus. After baptism we are no longer to eat and drink from the resources of this earth and its elemental forces, but we are to consume our life-supply only from Christ! He becomes our manna and our miracle, and the Holy Spirit leads us on into the dreams of God.

So, baptism is a water-marked passage from the old life to the new life in God, and it carries with it real outcomes and requirements. It is not just a ceremony, or a religious rite that we practice to join a group, or to become a member of a Church. We don't repeat it over and over as though we need additional cleaning, because we were made totally clean, and we were forgiven our sins when we trusted Jesus. Paul recounts his first encounter with Jesus and how Ananias said to him, "What are you waiting for? Get up and be baptized. Have your sins washed away by calling on the name of the Lord" (Acts 22:15–16). Baptism is something we do to obey Christ and begin our journey with him. Jesus commanded in the closing words of Matthew, "I have been given all authority in heaven and on earth. Therefore, go and make disciples of all the nations, baptizing them in the name of the Father and the Son and the Holy Spirit" (Matthew 28:18–19). We see from the words of Jesus that when we are immersed in obedience to Christ we are baptized into the Trinity. That is Christ's gift to us and the joy of his work on our behalf! We are restored into a relationship with all three members of the Godhead. Our Father who loves us takes us in. Jesus Christ our brother and savior embraces us in love. The Holy Spirit, God with us on this earth, wraps himself around us. We have left our old life behind, Christ has washed away all our sins when we put our faith in him, and we are on our journey with God in heavenly realms—the Kingdom of God. I have come to realize that any act of obedience to God will release God's power in our lives, and public baptism, in obedience to Christ, will release the power and presence of God all around us. Yes, I realize that baptism doesn't save us, our faith in Christ alone is what saves us, but we choose to be baptized in obedience to him in order to pass a simple test of faith and mature in him.

When we are baptized we show our submission to Christ. It is true the John the Baptist baptized people before Jesus had announced the Kingdom was here. John preached that people should turn away from sin, and self-righteousness, greed and religious pride and they should turn back to God. Those who agreed with him would get baptized by John to show they were repenting and in agreement with his message. John's message went on to say that by repenting the people could have their sins forgiven, and that they were to turn their attention toward the coming Messiah, the Christ. When Jesus arrived on the banks of the River Jordan to be baptized by John everything in creation must have paused to take notice, because at that moment everything changed. When Jesus' disciples begin to baptize new followers, John's baptism fades away. Jesus doesn't baptize us toward God, he baptizes us into God. Jesus doesn't baptize us toward the Kingdom, he baptizes us into the Kingdom. Jesus doesn't just baptize us out of sin, but also into the power to live righteously—in a whole new spiritual realm. His baptism is the one that is foreshadowed by Noah and Moses who went through water into a new life, but Jesus will also take us through fire. We will pass through fire because it destroys the old things with fierce perfection, and it prepares us for our new life with God as his Holy people. Fire is a purifying catalyst, and so we can add this picture to our understanding of being baptized. John knew this fiery baptism was coming when he said of Jesus, "He will baptize you with the Holy Spirit and with fire" (Matthew 3:11). The Holy Spirit is Holy God, and the fire of our baptism with Christ creates a purified place in us for the Presence of God to live. This is the one baptism that is listed here, "For there is one body and one Spirit, just as you have been called to one glorious hope for the future. There is one Lord, one faith, one baptism, and one God and Father, who is over all and in all and living through all" (Ephesians 4:4–6).

This passage from Hebrews 6:1-3 says we should be well versed in the "instructions about baptisms." Baptisms in this encouragement is plural. This is exactly what we have been learning already. The picture and process of being baptized has many examples and insights from the Scripture, but they all point to passing through an element from one place to another place.

However, because Ephesians 4 emphatically states there is only one baptism, some translators of the English Bible had written, instead, "instructions about ritual washings" in the Hebrews passage because they weren't sure if it was wise to translate baptisms in the plural. It is, however, easy to see that the instructions about Jewish ceremonial washings does not fit well in our elementary Kingdom teachings' list because that has nothing to do with maturing in Christ. Besides, learning how not to trust in religious rituals was covered in the teaching on "repenting from dead works." We need to read this in a very straightforward way: every believer should be clear on the basic lessons of the baptisms. Paul is aware that we need to understand the basics of the baptisms, including the baptisms of Noah through the flood, of Moses through the water and the cloud, of John the Baptist for repentance, of Jesus into the Trinity, the baptism of fire into the Presence of God, and the baptism of the Holy Spirit—which Jesus promised to all his disciples. All of these are baptisms, and each has a different story of death, burial and new life, but only in Christ can we be baptized into God. Only in Christ can we be resurrected to live forever with him. This is what the Ephesians passage is underlining because Ephesians is a book about our unity, our togetherness as one family.

Remember, we may be commanded to be baptized in water to show our obedience to Jesus, but Jesus is to baptize us with the Holy Spirit and with fire. This is different, even to a child, than just being baptized in water when we first choose to follow Jesus. We need to understand and receive his command with faith, "Do not leave Jerusalem until the Father sends you the gift he promised, as I told you before. John baptized with water, but in just a few days you will be baptized with the Holy Spirit" (Acts 1:4–5). This promise of the baptism with the Holy Spirit was lived out in many places in the New Testament accounts. Watch this drama unfold in Paul's journey from Acts 19:

> While Apollos was in Corinth, Paul traveled through the interior regions until he reached Ephesus, on the coast, where he found several believers. "Did you receive the Holy Spirit when you believed?" he asked them.
>
> "No," they replied, "we haven't even heard that there is a Holy Spirit."
>
> "Then what baptism did you experience?" he asked.
>
> And they replied, "The baptism of John."
>
> Paul said, "John's baptism called for repentance from sin. But John himself told the people to believe in the one who would come later, meaning Jesus."
>
> As soon as they heard this, they were baptized in the name of the Lord Jesus. Then when Paul laid his hands on them, the Holy Spirit came on them, and they spoke in other tongues and prophesied. There were about twelve men in all. (Acts 19:1–7)

When the Holy Spirit comes on us, when he fills us, when we are immersed in him things happen. It is fiery. It is powerful. We often speak in tongues, and we often prophecy. I have learned to always expect the power of God to come in a special way when anyone is baptized in obedience to Christ in water. I have also learned to expect the power of God to be released in a special way when believers trust the Lord for the baptism of the Holy Spirit.

This baptism in the Holy Spirit does require trust, it often requires asking, and sometimes it involves waiting. When the disciples obeyed Jesus and waited in the upper room in Jerusalem, "Suddenly, there was a sound from heaven like the roaring of a mighty windstorm, and it filled the house where they were sitting. Then, what looked like flames or tongues of fire appeared and settled on each of them. And everyone present was filled with the Holy Spirit and began speaking in other languages, as the Holy Spirit gave them this ability" (Acts 2:2–4). Remember, these believers had already been baptized in water in obedience to Jesus, they had walked with him in life, and seen him after the resurrection. After his resurrection Jesus had miraculously appeared to these disciples and, "Then he breathed on them and said, 'Receive the Holy Spirit'" (John 20:22). They had received the Holy Spirit as Christ blessed them with his Presence, but Jesus made clear, earlier, in John 14:17, as he spoke to these same disciples that, "he lives with you now and later will be in you." Jesus was excited about the time when the Holy Spirit would come in a miraculous new way to live inside of his people, and give them power for walking in Kingdom authority! It is not enough to assume on the Holy Spirit's company, it is our gift from God to receive him into the core of our lives as our power to live victoriously! This is the gift of the Holy Spirit that Jesus had announced. Though in our culture this teaching has taken some serious diminishment, the apostles were serious about it! Peter preaches, "Each of you must repent of your sins and turn to God, and be baptized in the name of Jesus Christ for the forgiveness of your sins. Then you will receive the gift of the Holy Spirit. This promise is to you, and to your children, and even to the Gentiles —all who have been called by the Lord our God" (Acts 2:38–39). It was serious business to the apostles to make sure when people were baptized in water and were putting their faith in Christ, that they heard about Christ's promise of the Holy Spirit: "When the apostles in Jerusalem heard that the people of Samaria had accepted God's message, they sent Peter and John there. As soon as they arrived, they prayed for these new believers to receive the Holy Spirit. The Holy Spirit had not yet come upon any of them, for they had only been baptized in the name of the Lord Jesus. Then Peter and John laid their hands upon these believers, and they received the Holy Spirit" (Acts 8:14–17).

We must first place our faith in Christ as our salvation because he reunites us with God. Being baptized in water is basic obedience in following him. Trusting Christ transforms us into a place for God to dwell. His gift to us, now, is the Holy Spirit to empower us for living from the eternal source with eternal power! We trust Christ, then, and ask him for the gift of the Holy Spirit which we are absolutely sure to receive! In Luke 11:11–13, Jesus says, "You fathers—if your children ask for a fish, do you give them a snake instead? Or if they ask for an egg, do you give them a scorpion? Of course not! So if you sinful people know how to give good gifts to your children, how much more will your heavenly Father give the Holy Spirit to those who ask him." We must ask the Father, and trust his good, giving heart, for the gift of the Holy Spirit. We must ask those who are confidently baptized in the Holy Spirit to lay their hands on us and have faith that God, who loves to give good gifts to his children, will have great pleasure in pouring out the promised and powerful Holy Spirit on our lives. This is in keeping with what we read earlier in 1 Corinthians 10:2, that the people who followed Moses were baptized in the "cloud and in the sea." The sea is like the waters of baptism and salvation, and the cloud is like the leadership and constant comfort of the Holy Spirit.

One time when Peter was preaching, "the Holy Spirit fell upon all who were listening to the message. The Jewish believers who came with Peter were amazed that the gift of the Holy Spirit had been poured out on the Gentiles, too. For they heard them speaking in other tongues and praising God. Then Peter asked, "'Can anyone object to their being baptized, now that they have received the Holy Spirit just as we did?' So he gave orders for them to be baptized in the name of Jesus Christ" (Acts 10:44–48). It's not the order of things—the perfect sequence of events—that is most important. That kind of thinking belongs to this world which obsesses over the right way, the perfect methods, and the approved rituals. The world doesn't understand the loving, personhood of God, either. The Holy Spirit is not a ceremony, he is a Person of God. We, instead of trusting our old mindset, choose to trust in God's word, and Christ's commands. We follow Christ in water baptism as he transports us into our new life in the Promised Land of his Kingdom, and we ask for the baptism of the Holy Spirit so we have the graceful power to live there.

We repent for thinking that God would lead us to a Kingdom that we did not have the power to live in! Receiving the Holy Spirit is not a religious system to get right, nor is it a puzzle about "how-much-of-God-did-we-get-when" that we need to figure out. It is, in short, enjoying the gift of God in the person of the Holy Spirit. He is not a ghost we are negotiating with, he is a person, and so we invite him into our lives. We ask him to fill us, to empower us, and to immerse us in his Presence! Jesus said, "And I will ask the Father, and he will give you another Advocate, who will never leave you. He is the Holy Spirit, who leads into all truth. The world cannot receive him, because it isn't looking for him and doesn't recognize him. But you know him, because he lives with you now and later will be in you. No, I will not abandon you as orphans—I will come to you" (John 14:16–18). The Holy Spirit comes in our lives so we won't be alone, so we won't think and live like orphans; so that we can understand right from wrong, and be wise in Kingdom things. The Holy Spirit covers us with power so we can be brought into family fellowship, be comforted and empowered, and guided though a life filled with boldness. All these things come from being filled with the Holy Spirit so it is time to say yes to our two baptisms, regardless of the order or the style in which they come: We will be baptized in water in obedience to Christ when we put our faith in him. We will also follow the apostles' example, and allow others to lay their hands on us and pray for the baptism of the Holy Spirit in our lives. One purifies us for the Presence of God, and the other empowers us for Kingdom living.

FAMILY VALUES

Improvisation is a musical ability that I adore, and, when it is built on a strong understanding of musical fundamentals, it can be beautiful. I have learned over the years, however, that improvisation should not be attempted by the musically immature, at least not in public, and certainly not past their mastery of the fundamentals. Music, of any kind, especially improv, will deconstruct if it is not built on a strong foundation in the fundamentals.

Musical improvisation is a lot like a romance. Romance is a spontaneous improvisation of affection between two people, but this affection must be built on the fundamentals of love, trust, and respect, or the romance will deconstruct. We have all read the story or seen the movie where youthful attraction leads to a passionate romance, but, predictably, it all falls apart when their love is tested. Romance that fails because of a weak foundation is a basic plot component of romantic tragedies. Without a foundation of love, respect, and trust, romance devolves into a sad, temporary thing. Romance, like music, can be beautiful, but it has to be built on a solid foundation.

Musical improvisation and romance have much in common with our relationship with God. Our affections for God—our worship, and our fellowship with one another as God's people—will be graceful and strong if we have the foundations in place to properly support it. In contrast, much of our walk with God and the community of faith will feel like an awkward, silly, musical improvisation if we have not mastered the more fundamental parts of our relationships.

Some of the fundamental things of living in Christ have been so neglected in modern times that they seem strange when we hear them for the first time. Like hearing an instrument we have never heard before, there are some teachings that we are not sure how to fit into the music of our lives. The phrase from Hebrews 6: *the laying on of hands*, may sound strange when we first hear it. This phrase sounds different than the basic teachings about Christ, repenting from evil deeds, placing our faith in God, or even, instructions about baptisms. Yet, it is in our list of the most elementary Kingdom fundamentals that every believer should know and be confident in. It is our work, now, to understand that this idea, the laying on of hands, which was no side-item for Paul, is to be a foundational element for all of us.

The maturity of a musician, we should note, is not built on being good at only one element in the fundamentals of music. There once was a man with only one string on his guitar. Wow, could he make it sing! Not distracted by the other five missing strings his proficiency on the one string was amazing. He could play lead, he could play grace notes and flowers, he could play the melody, but … he could never play the chords in a whole song. He could never give us the whole movement of a song, only parts of it, and so, as a guitar player, he was interesting, but he was not musically complete. When there was a band who needed a novelty they might call this guy, but if someone wanted to really hear beautiful music played they would have to go to someone else.

I may have been guilty in my life as a believer, and as a teacher, of occasionally playing one string for the attention it got me. My singular revelation about a single spiritual thing may have been novel, but it was not the whole Kingdom song. Many of us have played one interesting part of the Christian message down to a unique form of embellishment, but we are still having difficulty understanding the whole culture of the Kingdom of God. We cannot afford to leave out any teaching from our list in Hebrews 6, and expect to have a strong foundation in Christ. We must get a firm understanding of what this teaching about the laying on of hands really means, and place it firmly into the foundations of our lives.

The *laying on of hands* is, in short, the physical act of someone in authority putting his hands on someone else and transferring his authority, his blessing, and even his family lineage—his family connection—on to that person. In Numbers 27:18-20 Moses asks the Lord to appoint a suitable replacement for him as a leader over the people. He said to God, "'Please appoint a new man as leader for the community. Give them someone who will guide them wherever they go and will lead them into battle, so the community of the Lord will not be like sheep without a shepherd.' The Lord replied, 'Take Joshua son of Nun, who has the Spirit in him, and lay your hands on him. Present him to Eleazar the priest before the whole community, and publicly commission him to lead the people. Transfer some of your authority to him so the whole community of Israel will obey him'" (Numbers 27:16–20). Moses transferred some of his authority to Joshua, in public, by laying his hands on him and this commissioned Joshua into his season of leadership for the people of Israel. "Now Joshua son of Nun was full of the spirit of wisdom, for Moses had laid his hands on him. So the people of Israel obeyed him, doing just as the Lord had commanded Moses" (Deuteronomy 34:9). This is an amazing story and every Hebrew student of the Scripture knew it, so when Paul refers to the "laying on of hands" this picture of Moses and Joshua would have been one of the first pictures in his mind.

Another famous story in the Old Testament involves Joseph seeking his own father's blessing on his two sons. His father was Jacob (son of Isaac, son of Abraham). The way Jacob laid his hands on his grandsons, Joseph's sons, would establish the leadership line of the family, the heir of his authority, and the primary rights to his own family lineage. The story goes: "So Joseph brought the boys close to him, and Jacob kissed and embraced them … He [Jacob] put his right hand on the head of Ephraim, though he was the younger boy, and his left hand on the head of Manasseh, though he was the firstborn. … But Joseph was upset when he saw that his father placed his right hand on Ephraim's head. So Joseph lifted it to move it from Ephraim's head to Manasseh's head. 'No, my father,' he said. 'This one is the firstborn. Put your right hand on his head.' But his father refused. 'I know, my son; I know,' he replied. 'Manasseh will also become a great people, but his younger brother will become even greater. And his descendants will become a multitude of nations.'" (Genesis 48:13–19, excerpted). This is strange for us to understand in modern times, but it shows how important the act of laying hands on someone was in Hebrew family connections, and how it transfers certain authority and certain blessings to the sons. The right hand was the hand of authority. This is why it is said of Jesus that "he sat down in the place of honor at the right hand of the majestic God in heaven," in Hebrews 1:3. It is important to note that this blessing of the right hand was an intense, family-building expression.

Another picture we have of someone in authority laying their hands on another was in the life of Christ. Jesus often healed people, and when he did he often laid his hands on them. "No matter what their diseases were, the touch of his hand healed every one" (Luke 4:40). So famous were his healing hands that even Jewish leaders knew he had authority: "The leader of a synagogue came and knelt before him. Then a leader of the local synagogue, whose name was Jairus, arrived. When he saw Jesus, he fell at his feet, pleading fervently with him. 'My little daughter is dying,' he said. 'Please come and lay your hands on her; heal her so she can live'" (Mark 5:22–23). Healing is certainly a blessing. And healing certainly shows the one who is laying on hands has the authority to heal. When Jesus laid his hands on people he was showing he had the authority to heal, and that he had a familial love for those he touched. He did not want to heal from a distance, he wanted to touch us with his hands of love.

Even as the apostles preached the Gospel after Christ's death and resurrection they would call out to the Lord for his hand of healing to touch them, and for his authority to be known to the people. They prayed even while under great persecution from the unbelieving religious leaders, "'And now, O Lord, hear their threats, and give us, your servants, great boldness in preaching your word. Stretch out your hand with healing power; may miraculous signs and wonders be done through the name of your holy servant Jesus.' After this prayer, the meeting place shook, and they were all filled with the Holy Spirit. Then they preached the word of God with boldness" (Acts 4:29–31). Jesus has shared his authority to heal the sick with every believer, "They will be able to place their hands on the sick, and they will be healed" (Mark 16:18). He has also shared the authority to bless others with the empowerment of the Holy Spirit. The apostles placed their hands on those who had received Christ, and they were filled with the Holy Spirit and with new spiritual abilities. In Acts 8:17, 9:17, and 19:6 the Holy Spirit was poured out when believers, with authority, laid hands on people and prayed for them. Receiving the Holy Spirit is certainly a blessing, and it certainly comes from a heavenly authority. The outpouring of the Holy Spirit, I might add, contains the distinct endorsement of family connection. It is the Holy Spirit, you remember, that Jesus promised us so that we would not be left as orphans, and it is the Holy Spirit who is the Spirit of Adoption! So, now, we begin to see the simplicity of the meaning of the laying on of hands. It transfers authority, it contains blessings, and it builds our family connections. We might say it this way: the laying on of hands is an act of healing that transfers God's authority into our lives, that blesses us with gifts from God, and that unites us together as one family in him!

We should pause here and underline something very important. Many have made the mistake of thinking of the laying on of hands as primarily the idea of a healing touch. They see it as casual and relational, but they have not yet seen the intense connection that Paul was connecting to the story of Moses and Isaac when they laid their hands on Joshua and Joseph. This, in our elementary understanding, is the Kingdom way that authority and responsibility are established! Let's dig in to the basics of this elementary Kingdom teaching. In the life of the early Church there was only one path to higher responsibility in the community of faith. There was only one kind of touch that would give people the blessing and the authority they needed to work as leaders in ministry. There was only one thing needed to be commissioned and blessed into Christian service. Yes, it was the laying on of hands. Paul reminded Timothy about this moment in his life when he said, "This is why I remind you to fan into flames the spiritual gift God gave you when I laid my hands on you. For God has not given us a spirit of fear and timidity, but of power, love, and self-discipline" (2 Timothy 1:6–7). This "spiritual gift" that came when Paul laid his hands on him was certainly the power of the Holy Spirit, but it may have been a specific, new, gift empowering Timothy in his life as a leader. Paul reminds Timothy again in a different letter about a similar time: "Do not neglect the spiritual gift you received through the prophecy spoken over you when the elders of the church laid their hands on you" (1 Timothy 4:14). This may not be, as exampled in Timothy's life, a single event, but any occasion where a humble learner receives the authority, the blessing and a deeper family connection with leadership in the Church. It could be in a small family setting, or in a larger, more official ceremony, but the important part is the connection to family relationships who are able to impart something real and powerful through prayers of blessing and endorsement.

Paul and Barnabas were commissioned into ministry in the same way. In the book of Acts it says that some of the prophets and teachers in the Church in Antioch were praying together, and, "the Holy Spirit said, 'Dedicate Barnabas and Saul for the special work to which I have called them.' So after more fasting and prayer, the men laid their hands on them and sent them on their way" (Acts 13:2–3). They were already showing leadership, and they were already showing spiritual gifts, but they were not released into their next season of responsibility in ministry without their overseeing comrades laying their hands on them and commissioning them into it.

So what does all this say to us now in practical terms?

First, it is affirming something very simple. In the Kingdom of God we don't look to academic resumes to commission us into leadership. Study may equip us in many ways, but it is not the way we are to find a confident place in ministry responsibilities. Neither are our spiritual gifts the endorsements we need to lead others and do ministry work. Gifts are only spiritual tools, and though they are necessary for the power to do ministry, they are not how leaders are commissioned. In the Kingdom there is the absolute necessity for strong family connections and submission to those in authority. It is neither our degrees, nor our gifts that make us fit to lead and minister in the family of faith. It is neither our vision nor our experience that qualifies us to have authority in the Church. It is neither our passion nor our popularity that makes us fit for leadership in the work of the Kingdom. It is only the endorsement of family leadership through the laying on of hands that sets us in a confident place to serve the people of God.

Secondly, we can see that the laying on of hands is a contract which requires the recipient of the prayers and those doing the commissioning to trust one another. The laying on of hands requires deep humility in those who receive the prayers, because they are submitting to the endorsement of people, not institutions. Because it is not an organizational approval, but a personal endorsement of trust, the laying on of hands also requires those who practice it to be deeply acquainted with those they pray for. We must trust one another. When we are maturing in our faith we don't need a position in an organization to tell us when we are passing from childhood to adolescence. We need the adults in the family to come lay hands on us and say, "Well done. You are growing up." When it is time for us to take up adult level responsibilities in the Church we don't need to dazzle others with our spiritual gifts or show we can speak in public well. What we need is for the leaders in the Church to publicly show that they know us, that they love us, and that they trust us as leaders among the family of God. The laying on of hands is an affirmation of proximity between people and an agreement in their hearts. It establishes, in perfect Kingdom style, the very nature of our eternal community which is family— "fit together perfectly. As each part does its own special work, it helps the other parts grow, so that the whole body is healthy and growing and full of love" (Ephesians 4:16). This means that when we see people "quick-changing" their leadership in order to find a faster track to ministry assignments we can, and should, be suspicious of their immaturity. Paul says to each of us in 1 Thessalonians 5:12, "respect those who labor among you and are over you in the Lord and admonish you, and to esteem them very highly in love because of their work." This word respect he uses, referring to those who would lead us and watch over us, means to really see someone for the gift they are to us and to have a deep appreciation for them.

Practically speaking, we need a new instinct among both our leadership fraternities and our young leaders toward spiritual family endorsements. We need both overseers and students to look to family endorsement on the path of ministry readiness, rather than to their resumes in an organization which have given them a place, or to their dynamic gifts which have gained them attention. We have seen the instinct among leadership structures to promote those who are loyal, those who are useful, or those who can advance their cause with their gifts and charisma … this all represents terrible immaturity among the ranks of leadership. It is time to repent from this model we learned from the world, and to adopt a new model of submission that we received from Kingdom culture. The Kingdom of heaven is committed to holistic individual and family health. Every person in leadership must be firmly connected to this elementary value in the Kingdom, and must prove, through their connections with other family-minded leadership, that he or she is ready to carry on the work of equipping the people of God as a healthy family. What is going on in our present Christian community where everyone seems to be self-appointing, self-endorsing, and self-promoting themselves into leadership in the Church reveals a complete lack of understanding in this elementary Kingdom principle. This is why leaders leave "mentors," or "guides" for new ones as fast as they can have a disagreement with them. This is why Churches have begun to receive new leadership like they were hiring an employee instead of receiving family oversight. It is a terrible sign that things have gone terribly wrong, and that we have forgotten one of the most fundamental building blocks in Kingdom elementary school.

The Kingdom in its most elemental form is a family Kingdom. Matthew 13:43 says, "Then the righteous will shine like the sun in their Father's Kingdom. Anyone with ears to hear should listen and understand!" We long for a global Church community that would reflect this simple Kingdom value. We have grown so tired of a Church where people see the Kingdom as individual power, gifts, supernatural insight, visions, advocacy, or even having the right doctrine. We are also unimpressed with a Christian culture that seems to be defined by white papers, mission statements, executive leadership models, and organizational values. This is what people do when they feel they must do their best with what they have. Unfortunately, when we just look around this world and try to use what we see, we end up building with the elements from this world. Trying to create Kingdom culture with worldly elements creates dead works. Worldly thinking produces poor relationships, and it leaves wounded people in its wake. On the other hand, when we look to the Kingdom of heaven for the elements we need to live in Kingdom life, then we can build an eternal culture! Jesus explains in Luke 14:7-11, that he who looks to be first in this world, will be last in the Kingdom, but he who loves to serve others and wait on their invitations to serve in new ways, will be first in the Kingdom of God. This is why, in the Kingdom, we honor our fathers and mothers, and we never remove them from their place of leadership when we are taking up our own place of responsibility. In the deadly, worldly way of leadership advancement, we have often been guilty of patricide—the killing of our fathers—in order to make room for ourselves so we could take their place. This is not how a family works, and this is not, then, the way of the Kingdom!

In this simple, elementary Kingdom teaching we can imagine a healthy Church coming into being! We are all longing for believers who can name the beautiful people who laid hands on them and stirred up their spiritual gifts, because these kinds of believers can be trusted! We are longing for gifted ones who can wait for the approval of their oversight before launching themselves into positions of leadership, because these kinds of leaders can be trusted! We are also longing for leadership who can be paced and guided by their leadership, because these leaders will be paced and patient with us as well! When we have learned to romance the beauty of our family connections—our family unity —more than we romance our personal place and advancement, then we will be coming into the elemental ways of the Kingdom.

This is so fundamental, and so critical, that Paul told Timothy, as it related to commissioning people to do ministry work, "Never be in a hurry about appointing a church leader" (1 Timothy 5:22). What he said in more exact language was to never rush to lay hands on someone. The NASB translation says it this way, "Do not lay hands upon anyone too hastily and thereby share responsibility for the sins of others." Patience is the command, local testing is the process, and family endorsement is the final result. Let's choose to be careful and move along the lines of trust. It is important to learn that everything in the Kingdom moves at the speed of family relationships. Don't misunderstand: I am not saying that the Kingdom is subject to us, because that would imply that we are in charge of it. No, the Kingdom of God is an eternal, unchanging reality, and under the absolute authority of Christ, alone, but what I am saying is that our ability to participate in the Kingdom way is, indeed, subject to our ability to submit to right relationships. First, we must move at the relational pace that God has for us. Secondly, this pace will participate in loving connection with the beautiful people in our lives. We do not have any way to receive, or understand, the Kingdom in any way except as children might understand it, and children understand the whole world through the lens of their trusted relationships. Children participate in the truth, they do not pontificate about it. The God who loves us, and the people he has brought us into relationship with, are the literal places we will work out our Kingdom life—not in a revelation, a teaching, an understanding, or even a dispensation of power. The Kingdom is not received, nor is it practiced, in a relational vacuum. If we think otherwise, then we are preaching a Gospel that does not begin and end with the embrace of the Father who has loved us into his Kingdom through the life of his beloved son, Jesus, and empowered us to join him through the power of the Holy Spirit —all in a sweet, Triune, intimate, honor-filled relationship—with him and with one another!

ETERNAL LIFE

People aren't just born into Christianity through their natural families, like it is some kind of birthright from an earthly bloodline. Some religions present their membership in this way, but this is not how Jesus explains entering his Kingdom. He invites us to make a personal decision to follow him, and then we are miraculously born into a spiritual family, and connected to a heavenly culture. This book is an invitation to learn some very simple things about what it means to follow Christ into a heavenly culture. It is a culture filled with health and strength. Once we choose to follow Jesus we are on a life-long learning journey toward becoming whole and happy. With that in mind, let's continue to note some of the most basic, elementary things of following Christ. In Hebrews 6:1-3, our key passage for this short book, our next elementary teaching is *the resurrection of the dead.*

Coming back from the dead has taken on some gruesome roles in modern entertainment and movies. I think the recent zombie obsession is part of a twisted deception in the idea of being raised from the dead. It sounds just like something the enemy would do to distract us. In the Scripture we learn that our new bodies won't be disgusting like a zombie's body. No, and life after death won't be a time of mindless hunger and rage. It will be just the opposite! Being raised from the dead, as we learn in Kingdom elementary school, only happens through the power of Jesus Christ himself, is a gift to every believer, and results in a beautiful, eternal body that is fit for an eternal Kingdom! It is an eternal body that has all its hungers satisfied in Christ alone!

We are literally going to get new, eternal bodies!

The reason we are going to be resurrected from the dead and receive new bodies is related to the art of marksmanship. I recently found out that my father-in-law had received recognition in the military for marksmanship. This is a skill that requires some understanding of both the gun, and the trajectory of a bullet. A marksman not only knows where the bullet comes from, but where the bullet goes, and he carefully plans for all the forces that will affect the bullet in its flight so that it lands in exactly the right spot. The amazing part is that once he pulls the trigger, and the casing full of gunpowder explodes, that bullet is on its way and there is nothing he can do about it. It will go, along its planned trajectory, to the target it was intended for. Marksmanship is not built on feelings or complexities, but on a very clear, defined set of elementary physical principles. So it is with our trajectory in God.

God has made each of us special and beautiful. Sin and brokenness entered our world and influenced our trajectories for failure, every one of us. The Scripture says, "For everyone has sinned; we all fall short of God's glorious standard" (Romans 3:23). Missing the mark, or failing to reach the standard, describes why we so desperately need Jesus! The same passage goes on to say, referring to those of us who have placed our faith in Christ alone, "Yet God, with undeserved kindness, declares that we are righteous. He did this through Christ Jesus when he freed us from the penalty for our sins. For God presented Jesus as the sacrifice for sin. People are made right with God when they believe that Jesus sacrificed his life, shedding his blood" (Romans 3:24-25a). This is so wonderful. The Scripture clearly teaches that when we follow Christ we become new creations. When we place Christ as our Chief Cornerstone he transforms us into a new life.

We are literally made eternally alive in Christ the moment we place our faith in him, and as it says in Romans 6:4, "We died and were buried with Christ by baptism. And just as Christ was raised from the dead by the glorious power of the Father, now we also may live new lives." This new life begins as soon as we trust Jesus! At that very moment our eternal destiny is in him! It is just like being fired from a gun; once we enter our faith walk with him we are immediately on an eternal trajectory. We were destined for death, but now we are destined for a continuing life that we are already living now through Christ! We now understand that our resurrection from the dead is our perfect transition from this life to the next. Being resurrected from the dead in a new body is the unavoidable promise given to those who can no longer die, but must have new bodies in order to go on our eternal adventure in the family of God!

Jesus was the first to experience this new resurrected body that is promised to us as well. Jesus was resurrected from the dead, in a similar, but different, body. It was hard for the disciples to put all this together after they learned that Jesus was alive, but right in the middle of their troubled discussions, "Jesus himself was suddenly standing there among them. 'Peace be with you,' he said. But the whole group was startled and frightened, thinking they were seeing a ghost! 'Why are you frightened?' he asked. 'Why are your hearts filled with doubt? Look at my hands. Look at my feet. You can see that it's really me. Touch me and make sure that I am not a ghost, because ghosts don't have bodies, as you see that I do.' As he spoke, he showed them his hands and his feet. Still they stood there in disbelief, filled with joy and wonder. Then he asked them, 'Do you have anything here to eat?' They gave him a piece of broiled fish, and he ate it as they watched" (Luke 24:36–43).

After his resurrection Jesus sat there and ate fish in front of them! Never mind if he was hungry or not. Never mind what biological processes were being employed, he was actually eating fish! This means he was resurrected into a real physical body that could engage things in this world, but it also had new supernatural properties to it. We are going to have resurrected bodies like this, too! He had a real body that could be touched and seen as normal, but, amazingly, he still had the scars from his crucifixion that Thomas could put his fingers into. His body was also beyond the natural, because he could seemingly walk through walls and appear to them: "That Sunday evening the disciples were meeting behind locked doors because they were afraid of the Jewish leaders. Suddenly, Jesus was standing there among them! 'Peace be with you,' he said. As he spoke, he showed them the wounds in his hands and his side. They were filled with joy when they saw the Lord!" (John 20:19–20). Later when he ascended into heaven he was in a body that could fly, but it was also a body that could speak and interact with the disciples many times before he returned to the Father in heaven. The fact of Christ's resurrection, and his new body, continues to be emphasized throughout the lives of the apostles and their teachings. Paul writes, "He was buried, and he was raised from the dead on the third day, just as the Scriptures said. He was seen by Peter and then by the Twelve. After that, he was seen by more than 500 of his followers at one time, most of whom are still alive, though some have died. Then he was seen by James and later by all the apostles. Last of all, as though I had been born at the wrong time, I also saw him" (1 Corinthians 15:4–8).

The resurrection was even foreshadowed in the Old Testament. In Job 19:25-27 he says:

But as for me, I know that my Redeemer lives,
and he will stand upon the earth at last.
And after my body has decayed,
yet in my body I will see God!
I will see him for myself.
Yes, I will see him with my own eyes.
I am overwhelmed at the thought!

Daniel hears the Lord say, "Multitudes who sleep in the dust of the earth will awake: some to everlasting life, others to shame and everlasting contempt. Those who are wise will shine like the brightness of the heavens, and those who lead many to righteousness, like the stars for ever and ever" (Daniel 12:2–3). God always intended a resurrection so we could come into an eternal adventure with him! His love is so great! I am so glad to know that we are receiving a message of Kingdom life that has the power to conquer death! This is most fundamental to the Good News. Let's take a moment to think on those we love. Our parents, our husbands or wives. Let's think of our children. Some of them have already died. We will see some of them die in our lifetimes. Let's look at our own hands and feet. These will get probably get old, wrinkle, and then one day, if not from other means, each of our physical bodies will shut down and die. It is an inescapable fact, and it has haunted the human race since creation.

What does death really mean?

What does it say about us?

What happens next?

Is there life after this life?

I have cried many times in my life thinking of those I love who have died—or who I know will die one day—because I won't see them anymore in this life. My heart mourns their departure even before they are gone. I have been distraught at times thinking about my own death and how it may hurt others, or about how I will miss certain things in this life. Those who live with no hope for eternal life live in a kind of sad futility that can never be put to rest. Futility means that everyone comes to nothing, everything is useless. Many unbelievers do many things to try and make the futility go away, but it won't go because death always comes and puts an end to every argument, and every wish. The writer of Ecclesiastes saw this about life in the earthly realm and spoke about it frankly, but through our rebirth in Christ we now have life in the eternal realm. We do not cling to fatalism because it does not belong to us now that we are alive in Christ. Those of us who have put our hope in Christ have a totally different view of the future, and therefore a totally different view of our lives! In Christ, we have a radically different attitude, and it is the opposite of meaningless. Our life source is not here any longer, it is in heaven, in Christ, which has endless meaning! We don't have a death to fear any longer, but we have a miraculous resurrection to look forward to! We don't have to dwell in sadness any longer, nor do we have to live in futility! We can live in an eternal reality where everything comes to something, and everything can be useful!

We are definitely getting new bodies, but there is no way for certain to understand what they will be like, because they are going to be of heavenly origin, not made of this earth. Paul says it this way:

> But someone may ask, "How will the dead be raised? What kind of bodies will they have?" What a foolish question! When you put a seed into the ground, it doesn't

grow into a plant unless it dies first. And what you put in the ground is not the plant that will grow, but only a bare seed of wheat or whatever you are planting. Then God gives it the new body he wants it to have. A different plant grows from each kind of seed. Similarly there are different kinds of flesh —one kind for humans, another for animals, another for birds, and another for fish.

There are also bodies in the heavens and bodies on the earth. The glory of the heavenly bodies is different from the glory of the earthly bodies. The sun has one kind of glory, while the moon and stars each have another kind. And even the stars differ from each other in their glory.

It is the same way with the resurrection of the dead. Our earthly bodies are planted in the ground when we die, but they will be raised to live forever. Our bodies are buried in brokenness, but they will be raised in glory. They are buried in weakness, but they will be raised in strength. They are buried as natural human bodies, but they will be raised as spiritual bodies. For just as there are natural bodies, there are also spiritual bodies. The Scriptures tell us, "The first man, Adam, became a living person." But the last Adam—that is, Christ—is a life-giving Spirit. What comes first is the natural body, then the spiritual body comes later. Adam, the first man, was made from the dust of the earth, while Christ, the second man, came from heaven. Earthly people are like the earthly man, and heavenly people are like the heavenly man. Just as we are now like the earthly man, we will someday be like the heavenly man.

What I am saying, dear brothers and sisters, is that our physical bodies cannot inherit the Kingdom of God. These dying bodies cannot inherit what will last forever.

But let me reveal to you a wonderful secret. We will not all die, but we will all be transformed! It will happen in a moment, in the blink of an eye, when the last trumpet is blown. For when the trumpet sounds, those who have died will be raised to live forever. And we who are living will also be transformed. For our dying bodies must be transformed into bodies that will never die; our mortal bodies must be transformed into immortal bodies.

Then, when our dying bodies have been transformed into bodies that will never die, this Scripture will be fulfilled:

"Death is swallowed up in victory.

O death, where is your victory?

O death, where is your sting?"

For sin is the sting that results in death, and the law gives sin its power. But thank God! He gives us victory over sin and death through our Lord Jesus Christ. (1 Corinthians 15:35–57)

I realize that was a long Scripture to quote, but it was just too rich to miss any of it. It answers so many questions about our resurrection that I didn't want to paraphrase. Let's make it clear to one another! Let's teach our kids and share with our friends … we are looking forward to new bodies that will last forever! This is an amazing hope we have in Christ. This kind of hope is not based on a wish, but it is our promise from him. "And we believers also groan, even though we have the Holy Spirit within us as a foretaste of future glory, for we long for our bodies to be released from sin and suffering. We, too, wait with eager hope for the day when God will give us our full rights as his adopted children, including the new bodies he has promised us. We were given this hope when we were saved. (If we already have something, we don't need to hope for it. But if we look forward to something we don't yet have, we must wait patiently and confidently.)" (Romans 8:23–25).

So we are not just "hoping" for a body … we are guaranteed it!

Who else promises such a thing?

Only Jesus, and I am so thankful to him!

This is what we all really need: we need the message of the resurrection to come front and center in our elementary understanding of the Christian life. The cross is the gateway to it, but the resurrection is our vehicle to eternal life! It is not enough to recycle this world, we need to live into the next one. It is not enough to reform this world, we need to live into a brand new one. We were not made to suffer though this life in imperfect bodies, and just endure it with no answer—we have an answer in the resurrection! We can really say it aloud, "I am going to have a new body!" and that is a fundamental part of the Gospel.

My MaMaw, my dad's mom, had a high pitched voice, and it shook a little when she sang in her old age. I can still hear the excitement in her voice as I stood next to her in Church and she sang the old refrain, "I'll have a new body, Praise the Lord!" As a little boy this didn't make much sense to me, and I found more entertainment from the warble of her voice than the song itself. As of late, I have caught myself singing the same tune, and thinking of her in the next life already. When I think of my sons and my wife I want to sing that old song as well. How else can I deal with the hopelessness that loss can bring except through the promise of my resurrected body, and an eternal life that is real and has substance?

I have noticed that among the Christian "innovators" who try to pull the Kingdom down to an earthly level, and confine their good news to this realm—that ridiculing the hope of heaven is common on their lips. When I was in college we loved to make fun of the hymns about going to heaven because that, to us, belonged to the foolish escapists who had traded in a real Christian life for just a ticket to heaven. Well, something critical might be said about treating Christ like a ticket to heaven with no command to practice righteousness, sure, but I am sorry for mocking what is elementary to the Kingdom way of thinking: our literal resurrection to eternal life in heaven in new, but similar bodies, is of critical importance to a strong spiritual foundation.

Now Jesus explained that when we are resurrected we are no longer going to be married to one another, or get married again, but somehow I believe I will certainly know my sweet wife and love my sweet boys. Why not? Jesus knew his disciples when he returned and they certainly were able to know and love him. He ate fish with them, and he called them all by name! We will not lose our friends, but what we will gain in our new bodies and our eternal life in Christ will remove us from the way we have been in relationship in this world, and we will have a whole new, and even richer, way of relating to one another in love. This is a heart saving truth. I am so glad it is a fundamental truth, a first truth, in our understanding of Kingdom life. Paul was committed to having us all see it perfectly clear:

> And now, dear brothers and sisters, we want you to know what will happen to the believers who have died so you will not grieve like people who have no hope. For since we believe that Jesus died and was raised to life again, we also believe that when Jesus returns, God will bring back with him the believers who have died.

We tell you this directly from the Lord: We who are still living when the Lord returns will not meet him ahead of those who have died. For the Lord himself will come down from heaven with a commanding shout, with the voice of the archangel, and with the trumpet call of God. First, the Christians who have died will rise from their graves. Then, together with them, we who are still alive and remain on the earth will be caught up in the clouds to meet the Lord in the air. Then we will be with the Lord forever. So encourage each other with these words. (1 Thessalonians 4:13–18)

I am so encouraged with those words! I will no longer grieve over death without hope! Whether our earthly bodies go in the ground or meet him in the air, when he miraculously returns in global magnificence we will all be resurrected together at the same time. Now, to die means that we are somehow immediately in the presence of Jesus. "We are confident, I say, and would prefer to be away from the body and at home with the Lord" (2 Corinthians 5:8). Paul says, and again, "I am torn between the two: I desire to depart and be with Christ, which is better by far; but it is more necessary for you that I remain in the body" (Philippians 1:23–24). But Paul is not speaking of the resurrection because that comes later for us. When we die, before the resurrection of the dead, we who are believers have this confidence: we will go immediately and be with Jesus. When Jesus returns at the end of this age, and inaugurates the next, then all of us whose live with him will be resurrected into our new bodies! There does seem to be some time-warp stuff going on here, but we are not to worry about that at all. I know that my MaMaw has not yet been resurrected, but I know she is with the Lord. It is written that a thousand years can be like a day in the eternal realm with Christ.

Even those who died thousands of years ago who had faith in God, may be watching the time pass until the resurrection like it's just afternoon tea time.

PERFECT JUSTICE

Hebrews 6 reads, "Let us go on instead and become mature in our understanding." This is because there is such a thing as immature understanding. Maturity is not just the process of growing older, as we have already said, it is the process by which we become complete. The word in this passage is the word for complete or perfect, like we would consider a thing to be perfect when it is all we hoped it could be. My wife was born in Texas, and this makes her partly Mexican. Or at least it makes her Texican, which is an American who can cook Tex-Mex food to perfection. Every time she makes Tex-Mex food my two boys and I exclaim, "This food is perfect!" If things were not seasoned right, or if there was no smokey flavor on the meat, we would know it was not perfect, and we would wonder who had made dinner. What Robin does for southwestern cuisine is perfect. What God does in his plans for our lives is perfect as well. His plan for eternity is perfect. His plan for each of us is absolutely perfect. When Paul says in our key passage from Hebrews 6, that these simple teachings must be received and completely absorbed before we can become perfect, he was emphasizing that not one of them can be left out. Maturity is a picture of completion. To complete our list of elementary teachings we must add the last element. We must receive the Bible's teachings on eternal judgment.

I am so thankful that the elementary foundation stones of the Kingdom all fit together so closely, just like those little wooden blocks I had when I was a kid that had colorful ABC's and 123's stamped onto them. I am so glad that the elementary components of our faith are not big chunks of teachings that are separated by miles and miles of thinking. They are in simple shapes, close together, and easy to understand. In Kingdom elementary school we learn that eternity is not the same for everyone. We will also learn that it is not the same for every believer. This is great news for all of us. It means that our deep desire for justice will finally be satisfied. Many of us have deep commitments to the ideas of fairness, justice, and restoration in the world around us. The good news of God's plan is that perfect justice will be enacted, by Christ alone, at the end of this age.

At the end of this age, and before we enter the age to come, every Christian believer will be judged, each of us according to our works, before Christ. Some of us will be rewarded and some will not, and the different measures will all belong to Jesus' perfect judgment. It is called the judgment seat of Christ. Paul refers to this judgment when he says, "So we make it our goal to please him, whether we are at home in the body or away from it. For we must all appear before the judgment seat of Christ, so that each of us may receive what is due us for the things done while in the body, whether good or bad" (2 Co 5:9–10). There is a judgment for all of us as believers. We will stand before Christ and give an account for everything we have done, and receive what is due for our dead works or our eternal works.

Now, this teaching comes from the same apostle who has been so firm in teaching us that nothing can separate us from the love of God, and that our salvation in Christ is sure. That is not in question here. However, we find out that Paul is just as convinced that we will stand before Christ for a judgment of our lives that has real consequences. In this age it is difficult to teach this elementary truth, because everyone wants to think of themselves as existing on the same plane. Everyone wants to be equal in all things, and be given the same grade on every test regardless of their performance. Many read the Scriptures that explain how we are one in Christ, or all loved by God the same, and have simply made the conclusion that our eternities are all the same as well. We have learned to feel entitled to the same eternity regardless of our obedience or disobedience in this life. Some have even foolishly used the word "grace" to try and support this philosophy on an official level. Grace has come to mean a scoreless spiritual report card system where everyone gets an "A". It will not be like that at the judgment seat of Christ.

Because God's judgment is sure to come, and has real consequences, we should consider taking our lives seriously, like Peter said, "Since you call on a Father who judges each person's work impartially, live out your time as foreigners here in reverent fear" (1 Peter 1:17–18). It is time for every believer to take inventory of their lives right now, because judgment is coming. It is appropriate to fearfully consider the consequences of all our actions in this life—they are critically important. "For we will all stand before God's judgment seat … So then, each of us will give an account of ourselves to God" (Romans 14:10, 12, excerpted). We should make effort to put aside anything that holds us back from obeying God. We should commit to run away from all sin and earthly thinking, and set our minds on things above so we can make clear decisions about serving God. Just because our salvation was purchased by Christ without our participation, does not mean that we have been released from all responsibilities! The simplest definitions of the word maturity always includes responsibilities, and this book is about moving us all toward maturity. We are called to participate with him, now, by submitting our very lives to him, and taking up our responsibilities to which we are assigned.

Let's be clear, there is no shame at the judgment seat of Christ (Romans 9:33), and there is no condemnation (Romans 8:1), but there is still a judgment with consequences for every believer. We are not talking about the judgment between the righteous and unrighteous—that is a different judgment. Jesus said of that judgment: "Do not be amazed at this, for a time is coming when all who are in their graves will hear his voice and come out— those who have done what is good will rise to live, and those who have done what is evil will rise to be condemned" (John 5:28– 29). There are two judgments. At this point we are talking about the judgment where Christ judges his own people according to their deeds, whether good or bad. We have already discovered, in this little book, the way to understand if a deed is evil or if it is eternal. If we have lived from our eternal Kingdom source, then we will receive rewards! Paul says it this way, "If anyone builds on this foundation using gold, silver, costly stones, wood, hay or straw, their work will be shown for what it is, because the Day will bring it to light. It will be revealed with fire, and the fire will test the quality of each person's work. If what has been built survives, the builder will receive a reward. If it is burned up, the builder will suffer loss but yet will be saved—even though only as one escaping through the flames" (1 Corinthians 3:12–15). This passage shows us that we really can enter the next life with no reward from this life at all. This should inspire each of us to live in a way that would bring even more honor to God, and that would bring us rewards in the next life. We can now conclude that for everything in our life that had no connection to the eternal Kingdom, there is simply nothing added to us for eternity, however, for those who have invested in obedience to Christ and in the Kingdom life while on this earth—for them there will be eternal rewards added to their eternal life! This inspires each one of us to make a bold, and radical choice for God while we live in this world! We are on a heaven-bound journey where our source and our destination is the Kingdom of God, so we choose to live our lives in full-view of eternity.

Now, Jesus told another parable about a man who hired people to work in his fields. He hired them at different times in the day, but, "When those hired at five o'clock were paid, each received a full day's wage." This frustrated the other workers who were thinking their ideas of "fairness" had been offended. The one who owned the field says to them, "'Friend, I haven't been unfair! Didn't you agree to work all day for the usual wage? Take your money and go. I wanted to pay this last worker the same as you. Is it against the law for me to do what I want with my money? Should you be jealous because I am kind to others?' So those who are last now will be first then, and those who are first will be last" (Matthew 20:13b–16). Jesus is speaking to us in this passage about God's perfect justice, and our eternal contract with him. If Jesus says we are saved and given eternal life by trusting in him, then it is so. We don't get to choose if it is fair that he saves murderers, at the last minute, in the same way he saves nuns who have served him their whole lives. If Jesus says that our work will be judged and rewarded in the next life, then this is true as well. Whatever Jesus chooses, because all authority has been given to him, is now perfect justice for everyone and all of creation. Justice, after all, belongs to him. We simply get to submit to Jesus' perfect justice rather than our own!

It is very important to make Kingdom investments. A Kingdom investment is anything we spend in obedience to God. It is important to serve one another, to give generously, to love freely and to hear the Lord in everything because there is eternal reward for living this way. According to the Scripture, if we suffer on Christ's behalf there will be reward. If we are martyred for him there will be a reward. If we serve and love from a humble heart and do not seek self promotion in this world, then we will become greater in the Kingdom of heaven. On the other hand, if we promote ourselves and spend our life becoming great in this world, then we will not be promoted in the Kingdom of Heaven. We can't get around the fact that there will be levels of reward and places of honor in the Kingdom of Heaven. The Kingdom of Heaven is not an entitlement society. The judgment seat of Christ will put an end to the culture of entitlement forever. The first steps toward leaving an entitlement mindset is to begin to take responsibility for our own actions. We must discover God's assignments—God's expectations for each of us—and choose to be responsible in them. John 9:4, Acts 20:24, 1 Corinthians 3:5, 10:13, and 1 Peter 5:3 reveal that each of us has an assignment from God, regardless of its size or scope. Paul said, "Nevertheless, each person should live as a believer in whatever situation the Lord has assigned to them, just as God has called them. This is the rule I lay down in all the churches" (1 Corinthians 7:17 NIV). It is now to become our rule: we must obey God and invest our lives in the work of the eternal Kingdom!

Again, we are not talking about our righteousness or our eternal life because these are both gifts from Christ. Paul says of every believer that we will receive crowns of righteousness, "Now there is in store for me the crown of righteousness, which the Lord, the righteous Judge, will award to me on that day—and not only to me, but also to all who have longed for his appearing" (2 Timothy 4:8). This crown of life and a crown of glory are also mentioned in James 1:12, 1 Peter 5:4 and Revelation 2:10. We know that we have eternal life, but there really is an end to this world and a beginning of the next, and we must choose to live in this world like we are truly accountable to the next. We must overcome the fear of how we are judged in this world. What this world thinks of us does not matter. We must fear the judgment in the next world because it does matter. We must live with our hearts and loves firmly committed to our heavenly destiny, and give up on preserving our reputations for this world.

Everything counts, let's live like it.

Peter gives us this charge:

> Above all, you must understand that in the last days scoffers will come, scoffing and following their own evil desires. They will say, "Where is this 'coming' he promised? Ever since our ancestors died, everything goes on as it has since the beginning of creation." But they deliberately forget that long ago by God's word the heavens came into being and the earth was formed out of water and by water. By these waters also the world of that time was deluged and destroyed. By the same word the present heavens and earth are reserved for fire, being kept for the day of judgment and destruction of the ungodly.
>
> But do not forget this one thing, dear friends: With the Lord a day is like a thousand years, and a thousand years are like a day. The Lord is not slow in keeping his promise, as some understand slowness. Instead he is patient with you, not wanting anyone to perish, but everyone to come to repentance.
>
> But the day of the Lord will come like a thief. The heavens will disappear with a roar; the elements will be destroyed by fire, and the earth and everything done in it will be laid bare.

Since everything will be destroyed in this way, what kind of people ought you to be? You ought to live holy and godly lives as you look forward to the day of God and speed its coming. That day will bring about the destruction of the heavens by fire, and the elements will melt in the heat. But in keeping with his promise we are looking forward to a new heaven and a new earth, where righteousness dwells. (2 Peter 3:3–13)

Jesus is returning. Things are not going to stay the way they are for much longer. We must live with this always present in our imagination. Eternal judgment does not cause us to fear in anxiety of punishment, because there is no punishment for those of us who are in Christ. "There is no fear in love. But perfect love drives out fear, because fear has to do with punishment. The one who fears is not made perfect in love" (1 John 4:18). However, the judgment seat of Christ does motivate us to stay awake to the Holy Spirit's leading, and to not become lazy in this life. We pray like this:

I have put my faith in Christ and my future is certain in him, so I continue to take stock of my life, and seek counsel from my spiritual family on right living and right Kingdom investment. I also know that Jesus loves me, and that he does not pour out shame even though he knows every broken thought in my mind (Romans 2:16), so, I am so interested in pleasing him that I continue to work to purify my mind and make my life a happy place for the Holy Spirit to dwell! I know that he will reward me only according to what, in my life, was of eternal value, and so I have set my face toward eternal things. God help me, and help all of us, to seek first the Kingdom of God! I know without a doubt, that Christ's judgments are true (Romans 2:2), and whatever he decides will be just. "God will repay each person according to what they have done. To those who by persistence in doing good seek glory, honor and immortality, he will give eternal life" (Romans 2:6–8).

There is another judgment, but it is not for believers. It comes after the judgment seat of Christ, and is often called the second judgment because it is connected to what the Scripture calls the second death. This is an eternal judgment and a death that believers will have no part in. "Whoever has ears, let them hear what the Spirit says to the churches. The one who is victorious will not be hurt at all by the second death" (Revelation 2:11). "Blessed and holy are those who share in the first resurrection. The second death has no power over them, but they will be priests of God and of Christ and will reign with him for a thousand years" (Re 20:6). This is all very hard for any of us to understand. It is hard for us to imagine. The second judgment the Scripture clearly outlines is between believers and unbelievers, sheep and goats, wheat and weeds, the righteous and the unrighteous. It, too, takes place at the end of this age and it is called the Great White Throne of judgment. It is reserved for those who do not trust Christ. The Scripture teaches there are two phases for life after death for those who don't trust God. It teaches that believers who die will go immediately to be with the Lord, but unbelievers who die go immediately to a different place. This place is not heaven, and it is not a place of peace—it is called the realm of the dead, Sheol, the pit, and Hades. Quoting from the Psalms of David, Peter says, "Seeing what was to come, he [David] spoke of the resurrection of the Messiah, that he was not abandoned to the realm of the dead, nor did his body see decay" (Acts 2:31). This passage refers to a place where the dead reside without hope. This place could not hold Jesus—therefore it can't hold those of us who have our lives in him! In the Old Testament this place is called Sheol. Ezekiel 17 speaks about this realm as the pit—the realm of the unrighteous dead who are all together in one place. When Jesus told the story of Lazurus and a rich man, two men with different destinies, he referred to the same place as Hades when he said, "The time came when the beggar died and the angels carried him to Abraham's side. The rich man also died and was buried. In Hades, where he was in torment, he looked up and saw Abraham far away, with Lazarus by his side. So he called to him, 'Father Abraham, have pity on me and send Lazarus to dip the tip of his finger in water and cool my tongue, because I am in agony in this fire'" (Luke 16:22–24). There was a separation between these two men that could not be crossed. One was in the presence of peace, and one was in torment. This, however, is not what is seen in the Bible as hell even though Lazarus spoke of fire. Hell comes later, and it is what we see in the Scriptures as the second death reserved for the wicked. Jesus spoke of hell as a place the Jews knew as Gehenna, a trashed-out valley near Jerusalem, where idolatry was once practiced. It had become a place to dump and burn the city's trash. It was not a waiting place, it was a place where things come to an end. Jesus often taught this picture of a more final, and more terrible place than Hades where everything that was wicked would eventually be sent for destruction. This idea of the destructive, final future for the unrighteous becomes more specific when we read Revelation 20:

> Then I saw a great white throne and him who was seated on it. The earth and the heavens fled from his presence, and

there was no place for them. And I saw the dead, great and small, standing before the throne, and books were opened. Another book was opened, which is the book of life. The dead were judged according to what they had done as recorded in the books. The sea gave up the dead that were in it, and death and Hades gave up the dead that were in them, and each person was judged according to what they had done. Then death and Hades were thrown into the lake of fire. The lake of fire is the second death. Anyone whose name was not found written in the book of life was thrown into the lake of fire" (Revelation 20:11–15).

And then he concludes with words from Christ:

He said to me: "It is done. I am the Alpha and the Omega, the Beginning and the End. To the thirsty I will give water without cost from the spring of the water of life. Those who are victorious will inherit all this, and I will be their God and they will be my children. But the cowardly, the unbelieving, the vile, the murderers, the sexually immoral, those who practice magic arts, the idolaters and all liars— they will be consigned to the fiery lake of burning sulfur. This is the second death" (Re 21:6–8).

This is called the Great White Throne of judgment. It is, quite obviously, different from the judgment seat of Christ reserved for believers. I realize that everyone hates the idea of hell. I do, too. I wish it would just go away. No one wants to talk about it. Neither believers, nor unbelievers, ever want to bring it up. The only exception I can think of is when I was in middle school I remember it was popular to yell at other kids who hit you, or stole from you, and say, "You are going to hell!" Which, of course, in the South, meant we were fixin' to argue about who was going to hell, or not, for so long that we would forget why anyone brought it up in the first place.

Sometimes I wish that Jesus or the apostles would have just turned to the side and said something like, "This hell business is just breaking my heart." Somehow I think that we all just want to hear a little sympathy attached to these Scriptures about two, separate, eternal destinies so we won't feel so mean. We want to hear Jesus say to us, "Your sin and the idea of eternal punishment is just killing me..." and in that moment we realize it did kill him. Jesus died on a cross as a result of his pain and heartache over the prospect of hell. Jesus, who was God in the form of a man, died as a result of his sympathy and love for us. Rather than just having sympathetic feelings, however, he put his love into action and made a way for everyone to be saved and have eternal life through his horrific, love-proving death, and then his victorious resurrection! Just by trusting in him—just by calling out to Jesus to save us, the Scripture says, we will be saved. This is so simple, so wonderful: that anyone, anywhere, can have eternal life in a moment, but they still have to believe in him!

Sometimes I think we really just want to get the inside information that hell—wink, wink—is just a motivation tool. On one hand we want hell to be a casual myth used to help us along, but then again who wants to follow a savior who tells stories about being thrown into hell only to find out it was just a manipulative joke? I don't think Jesus would ever treat us that way. He does miracles, he does not do tricks. We would also never believe that Christ was condescending to a foolish belief system the Jews made up, or that the apostles were just gullible and foolishly went along with it. Eternal judgment is a foundational teaching in the basic elements of the Kingdom. One popular explanation for heaven and hell these days tries to develop a future-philosophy where there is no punishment for sin anymore because Jesus has really saved everyone in the world to heaven by his death. This philosophy explains itself by asserting that some are saved more than others by choosing to follow him in this life. Where in the Scripture do we find this teaching? When did this multi-level salvation era begin? Is this the end of our hope for justice? What is the point of the word "save" in this novel idea? What do we do with John's Revelation in chapters 20 and 21? I realize that these things John writes about are terrible, and no one likes them. If we argue with them, however, we find ourselves worse off than we were before—our feelings don't change the facts, but if we change the facts to suite our feelings then everything falls apart.

I do realize that there are many uncertainties in this conversation. I realize we have many unresolved questions circulating around this teaching. I realize there are questions around the innocence of infants and those who never heard the Gospel preached. I also realize there are arguments proving no one in the world is innocent. Many people do get trapped in these kinds of dilemmas. I can just hear the snake asking his favorite question over and over again: "Did God really say?" The devil is desperate to have us descend into either questioning or defending God's heart. God needs neither, and we won't produce anything eternal by questioning his heart, or trying to defend it. Both lead to confusion. I have chosen not to allow my uncertainties to rule over my confidences. For everything I am not sure about, there are a hundred things, through his Word, that I am absolutely sure about. I know that Luke 12 paints a very clear picture for us. Jesus, himself, speaks of the judgment of the world, and the fact that this judgment comes through him. He said in many different ways that he would divide, he would separate, he would judge the righteous from the unrighteous, and that we should pay more attention to our eternal consequences than to our comforts in this world. Sometimes I have to ask myself a clarifying question: Am I a sheep or a goat? I confidently answer, I am a sheep. I know this because I follow Christ. Sheep follow their shepherd, they don't just wander the earth eating whatever they see. I have decided to follow Jesus, and not just wander around doing whatever I want to do. Then I make a sheep noise for emphasis, Baaah. Since I am a sheep, I choose not to make any arguments about the existence or purpose of goats. That is outside of my understanding. I have eternity on my mind. I will not fall into the enemy's trap of participating in arguments that produce nothing for eternity. This may sound too simple, but, for me, it is where I rest. Here is how Jesus affirms my choice in John 3:18-21: "There is no judgment against anyone who believes in him [Jesus, referring to himself]. But anyone who does not believe in him has already been judged for not believing in God's one and only Son. And the judgment is based on this fact: God's light came into the world, but people loved the darkness more than the light, for their actions were evil. All who do evil hate the light and refuse to go near it for fear their sins will be exposed. But those who do what is right come to the light so others can see that they are doing what God wants."

In the elementary school of the Kingdom we must humbly cling to the fundamentals. We need to let the Scripture conquer us in this: There is a judgment for both believers and unbelievers. I will leave the details to the Lord in whom I have put my trust. This elementary teaching must be placed as a simple foundation stone in our lives, and not pushed aside like a big ugly rock we have no use for. It is a simple, foundational block. It has smooth sides, and it fits right beside "faith in God," "teachings about baptisms," and the "resurrection" as an elementary lesson in our walk with God. The judgement will be a beautiful time for those who believe. We look forward to it as God's way to make all things right, and to bring everything into his perfect order.

God's perfect love has cast out fear, but we also fear the Lord out of respect and don't feel that we should argue with him about the rest of eternity. One person can be thankful for gravity while it holds him safely on the ground. It allows him to walk around, and for every normal physical thing in life to work properly. Another person might curse gravity because his loved one fell off of a building. Is gravity, then, a blessing or a curse? We do not say that it is either. Gravity is simply a fact. How we choose to submit to it decides whether or not we are helped or harmed. I think the question we should be asking ourselves about the judgments of God has nothing to do with whether they are good or bad. They are both simply facts. Our question is how will we choose to submit to them. This elementary lesson is about our own heart to choose to agree with God. Eternity is always about what we have chosen to do in obedience to God. Eternity never puts God on trial. God has established perfection in his plan for all of creation. He planned it in his perfect love, and this perfection involves eternal judgment. I have chosen to believe that God loves me, I have chosen to follow Christ, and therefore his gravity—his judgment—is now a blessing to me. If some are crushed by his gravity, because they won't receive his love, then I have no ability to speak to it or understand it, but God is not on trial. When Job was suffering and asked God to defend himself did God feel obligated to explain his actions to him? In the end of that story Job proclaimed that God was God, and that Job was a man, and there was no further need for arguments. Job made a choice to trust God through his questions, not in spite of them. It makes no sense to me why anyone in all of history would willingly jump off of a building and then be angry at gravity, nor does it make any sense for us to rage against the judgment we learn about in the Scripture. We are to submit to it, and let this fact shape our lives toward maturity in Christ.

Now it is time for us to treat every moment in this life like it really counts. Every precious soul around us is worthy of love. Every person in this world, whether we agree with them or not, is worthy of a touch of dignity because God loves them. As his sons we will open our hearts to every one and express the heart of love and the message of an invitation to the eternal Kingdom through Christ. We will not give any credence to other gospels, and we will not fear the public's whip of ridicule when we lift up the cross of Christ as our gateway into eternal meaning. When unbelievers accuse us of being judgmental we just realize they don't understand John 3 that Christ did not come to judge but to save the world, but those who rejected him have judged themselves. We should not take this personally because we have chosen not to judge them either, but the very presence of Christ brings eternal conflicts into the atmosphere. We will choose to love without prejudice, and we will touch the broken among us with dignity. Because Christ lives in us, the light of the world, we will not be received by all men regardless of how much we love them. We must now choose to do away with preserving our own lives. We must not get caught up in self-preservation or in defending ourselves. Paul says, "We have only one judge and it is Christ. I care very little if I am judged by you or by any human court; indeed, I do not even judge myself. My conscience is clear, but that does not make me innocent. It is the Lord who judges me" (1 Corinthians 4:3–4). In Christ we have our perfect final judgment.

On him we build our lives, and to him we look for approval in everything.

SIMPLE

We have now completed our review of all the elementary teachings in Hebrews 6:1-3. We have learned that to become strong and mature in God, we must first learn the elementary teachings about Christ. We have engaged the command to turn away from dead works, and place our faith in God. We have reviewed the most basic instructions about baptisms, the laying on of hands, the resurrection of the dead, and eternal judgment. The promise of the Scripture is that if we understand this short list of teachings, and learn to walk in them, then we will be able to move forward to further understanding. We will become more mature as believers, and then be able to lead and teach others. This means if we have not received these simple truths, then we have not been maturing in Christ, we should not have tried to understand higher things in Kingdom life, and we should not be leading others. This should sound very natural and normal to us. Jesus comes to us and says, simply, "Follow me." He does not say, "Argue with me," or "Consider some of the things I will teach you." We remind ourselves that Jesus comes to each of us and asks us to exercise a simple, childlike trust, and to follow him in his footsteps.

The word pictures we have used to dig into these elementary teachings have been diverse. *Masonry* helped us see the importance of the cornerstone in the construction of a foundation, and that Christ is our only cornerstone. *Map* reading became a simple way to consider our true spiritual GPS—which is now heavenly—and repent from dead works sourced from this world. We learned that noticing the simple facts in front of us was necessary before we could understand the *mystery* of faith, and learn to trust in the heart of God. Since we are to grow strong and mature we used the simple goodness of *milk* as an illustration of the basic nutrition in God's Word. We learned that to engage in higher learning we must, first, understand the most basic elements of *math*—including the simple elements of the baptisms. We reviewed the fact that to perform a beautiful song we must be confident in the fundamentals of *music,* and we compared it to being confident in the fundamentals of family relationships. *Marksmanship* helped us draw a fast picture of understanding the resurrection as part of our eternal destiny, and the idea of *maturity* helped us consider building a complete set of teachings—including eternal judgement—rather than a partial set of comfortable electives in our Kingdom understanding. Every one of these word pictures has something in common, and it is not just the alliteration. Each one of these word pictures points us to the same conclusion. They all show how important the most elementary things are in building a whole and healthy life.

These days our spiritual strength is being challenged all the time. Our simple trust in God is being pressed on from every side. These are difficult times. It seems, to me, that we are in the very situation Paul was warning Timothy about when he writes, "Be prepared, whether the time is favorable or not" (2 Timothy 4:2). These are not easy days to follow Jesus. It is not a favorable time for speaking to others about our faith in him. It is getting harder and harder to share the Scriptures with others without being made fun of, and it is almost impossible to believe there really is a right and a wrong—everything is now somewhere in the gray middle. Of course we need help to deal with the pressures of life, but many of our recent solutions seem to be leaning away from the elementary things in the Scripture, and leaning toward secrets and insights from the world and its evolving mythologies. A myth is a story people think up for themselves to try and explain things they don't understand. This culture of mythology, where everyone designs their own explanations for life, is now so very popular with entertainers, academics, and even popular leaders in the Church, that it has become almost impossible for us to see past the confusing smoke of it all into the simple things the Scripture teaches about our life in God. We are having trouble keeping a clear mind, just like Paul noted to Timothy, when he said, "But you should keep a clear mind in every situation. Don't be afraid of suffering for the Lord. Work at telling others the Good News, and fully carry out the ministry God has given you" (2 Timothy 4:5). As a result we have grown fragmented in our thinking, and weak in our faith. But Paul continues to challenge Timothy like this: "Patiently correct, rebuke, and encourage your people with good teaching. For a time is coming when people will no longer listen to sound and wholesome teaching. They will follow their own desires and will look for teachers who will tell them whatever their itching ears want to hear. They will reject the truth and chase after myths" (1 Timothy 4:1-3). Apparently, our ears have been itching for a better, more popular, Christianity, and we have been very willing to tickle one another with the latest versions. Our problem is that with every innovation in Christian teaching we seem to have become a bit weaker as a people.

It usually does not take us long to outline awkwardness that exists in some of our modern Christian communities. The point of this book, however, was not to try and outline all our troubles, but to point clearly to a solution. It is now time for us all to consider returning each of these foundational truths to their rightful place in the ground floor of our spiritual lives. The challenge for us is to return to the simplest truths in the Word, and to abandon our adoption of more modern, more complex, and more shallow ways of living. It is time to return to deep and simple.

Most of us can take stock of our own lives and find examples of weakness and difficulties in our walk with God. Most of us can identify failures under pressure, or collapse in the face of hardships. But! We should not accept defeat as though it is normal for us! Who taught us that following Christ is just a way to barely survive this life? The apostles would be shocked to hear us speak to one another in this way, and they would be appalled at what we have begun to look to for our strength. Listen to James speak to us about our unavoidable hardships, "Dear brothers and sisters, when troubles come your way, consider it an opportunity for great joy. For you know that when your faith is tested, your endurance has a chance to grow. So let it grow, for when your endurance is fully developed, you will be perfect and complete, needing nothing" (James 1:2-4). Does it sound like he would be happy to just lay down and give up in the face of his problems? Does it sound like he is going to look anywhere else but to God for his help? James accepted trouble, yes, but he did not accept defeat! James saw troubles as a natural pathway through which we could gain strength in our spiritual lives!

Peter did not forget the simple things about God's heart, either, and he seemed very confident, just like James, when it came to trusting God through every difficulty. In his letter to believers who were suffering he said: "So be truly glad. There is wonderful joy ahead, even though you have to endure many trials for a little while. These trials will show that your faith is genuine. It is being tested as fire tests and purifies gold—though your faith is far more precious than mere gold. So when your faith remains strong through many trials, it will bring you much praise and glory and honor on the day when Jesus Christ is revealed to the whole world" (1 Peter 1:6-7). He was speaking as one who had personally suffered, to those he personally loved. Peter did not deny suffering, but he did deny defeat! Listen carefully: Peter did not need God to prove himself, no, quite the opposite, Peter was looking for a chance to prove himself to God! Peter was absolutely certain that God's promises were true regardless of the circumstances, and that God's purposes were trustworthy.

The apostles had a kind of trust that could shake down even the most horrific circumstances and rise up against their worst enemies. Listen to Paul! When Paul recounted his own difficult life he listed five beatings with whips, three with rods, one stoning, three shipwrecks, street robberies, cross-cultural threats, starving, freezing, and still he says, "So now I am glad to boast about my weaknesses, so that the power of Christ can work through me. That's why I take pleasure in my weaknesses, and in the insults, hardships, persecutions, and troubles that I suffer for Christ. For when I am weak, then I am strong" (2 Corinthians 11:9b-10). Paul stood up in the face of all kinds of pain and trials and confidently proclaimed that it was his pleasure to endure them because he was growing stronger through them! He was confident in God's heart, and confident in God's plan for his life.

We can have the confidence of James, Peter and Paul if we build our lives on the same truths they considered to be absolutely elementary in their journey with God. Seriously, this is the moment we have all been waiting for! If we become intimately acquainted with God's most basic promises and most basic teachings, we can become strong just like the great people we have read about in Scripture. We must choose, right now, to memorize and name aloud every basic teaching from this short passage of Scripture in Hebrews, then we can walk in them one step at time. This is exactly how the apostles became so strong, and it is exactly how we can become strong as well! The apostles had chosen to agree on the elementary things, and they placed them at the base of their walk with God. This built them up in a way that they could literally find pleasure in being challenged to the very edge of their strength!

I am very excited because we only have to make one simple, courageous choice: We can submit, and let the word of God conquer us in its deep simplicity, or we can push back and try to conquer the Word of God. If we choose to let the Word conquer us, then, I believe with all my heart, that we will receive all of its rewards. All of God's foundation stones are simple, smooth sided, and easy to put into place if we will only choose to submit to them. We must move on from an immature infatuation with one of the foundation stones, while neglecting the others as unimportant. It is time for us to embrace every single one of them as our most elementary spiritual building blocks, and as our favorite teachings! This is more than a poetry of word pictures. This is the most practical and personal stuff of life. I have personally witnessed a tragedy working itself out in the lives of those who have refused the whole of these elementary teachings. I have seen many fail to embrace these simple elements, and as a result have created weaknesses in themselves and the communities of believers gathered around them. In real life, many of us have seen countless "scholars" and "teachers" working so hard to conquer the Bible's stark simplicity, because its simplicity is so difficult. It's as though they want to say to their followers, "See, this is not that hard, this is not as bad as you thought, here is how I solved it for you." We should not follow them because weakness is already growing in their gardens. When we begin to agree with the elementary things of the Kingdom, without compromise, we will all learn that we are "not of this world" (John 18:36), and that to live in Kingdom culture is to live in opposition to the world. It is difficult, but it is worth it! As believers we will not fit in to popular streams of thought in the modern world, but if we submit to these Kingdom things there will be higher and higher places to go with God!

Just as Paul says in Hebrews 6, there really are higher things to move onto in our learning journey with Christ. There really is some spiritual calculus and advanced physics happening in the Kingdom of God, but first we must let Jesus open our minds to the simplicity of the Scriptures and the elementary things of the Kingdom. I submit to you, in conclusion, that we simply can't understand or enjoy any higher learning in the Kingdom until we have the elementary things in place. My position is to pray, and I would invite you to join me:

> "Holy Spirit, I ask you to teach me and lead me into all truth, but first build in me a rested confidence in the elementary things of the Kingdom.
>
> "If the simple word of God is hard, so be it.
>
> "If it opposes the world around me, so be it.
>
> "If it is contrary to my own feelings, so be it.
>
> "If it creates problems with my present intellectual math, and makes me uncomfortable, then I say this is the best way to live—in discomfort. I would rather suffer with your Word pressing down on top of me, and live in great discomfort, than to be caught trying to sweep your Word into a nice pile of "essence" teachings that cause me no more difficulty. I would be suspicious of my own heart wanting to pick and

choose what it liked and didn't like, so, 'Search my heart, oh, God, and mature me from the inside out!'"

DEEP

In a final, critical, encouragement, we must take into account that believers, everywhere, have started using words and ideas that really do belong to the culture of the heavenly realm, but these ideas are still, quite frankly, over their heads. We say this because these words aren't being handled with care. These words represent the depth and simplicity found in the Kingdom, but in modern times they are being used in shallow and complex ways. These heavenly terms have been thrown around so loosely in modern times, that our only conclusion is that some have learned the language of higher things, but have not yet learned the fundamentals. These popular, trending, words might include:

Community.

Kingdom.

Sonship.

Grace.

Apostle.

Ministry.

Family.

Justice.

This evolution of Christian terminology is popular now in books, blogs, and sermons, but this doesn't seem to be followed by an uptick in our strength and maturity as a community. We are witnessing a Christian culture that has not learned the simpler foundations listed in Hebrews 6, and, therefore it has been creating some pretty silly sounding improvisations, on one-string guitars, using these words. In addition, we have seen mature leaders growing so tired of the foolishness being attached to these terms that they have developed a suspicious twitch when anyone brings them up. Some leaders have been so disappointed by the immature misuse of this vocabulary, that censorship is their first instinct. We are in a dangerous place between untested license and universal restriction in the use of these precious words. Lord, please help me to not lose heart as I endure the misuse of these beautiful Kingdom concepts. I want to be clear about how each one of these words is being mishandled today:

> *Community* has come to replace the beautiful word Church, or the message of the eternal Kingdom. We are now satisfied to preach the gospel of shared life in this world, and that gospel often has little requirements placed on it from the eternal world in heaven. This word has become so earth-focused that we won't hear much about the resurrection from the dead or the judgment seat of Christ when being taught the gospel of community.
>
> *Kingdom* has been reduced to the earthly demonstration of spiritual power. It has become the buzz-word to draw people to conferences, regardless of what is being proclaimed. The elementary teachings from Hebrews 6 are often missing from this kind of Kingdom teaching today because it has become whimsical and flexible rather than eternal and permanent, and it no longer refers to God's family Kingdom that has been established in perfection in the eternal realm.
>
> *Sonship* has become a kind of permission to live free of any authority, and have no responsibility to the Church. It has been attached to a reckless idea of freedom which carries no requirements, no lineage, no responsibility—only license. Waiting on the laying on of hands has not yet been received

by many who preach sonship today, because they are not willing to submit to the family of God and the pace of ordered relationships.

Grace now means any way you like it, and is no longer connected to the simplest teachings of Christ, the only way. It no longer carries any clear requirements for righteous living. It has come to mean the ability to ignore much of the Bible because it seems too hard to reconcile to the niceness of God. The baptism in the Holy Spirit and the power to live and practice righteousness is not very popular in this new kind of "grace" culture.

Apostle has become a new notch up the leadership totem pole. It belongs to the leaders of mega-Churches or those who administrate large networks. Rather than receiving it as a servant role to lay the simple foundations of Christ in every believer's life, many new "apostles" prefer the accolades of the finished work and promotions to higher positions of management—the opposite of advancement in Kingdom culture.

Ministry means whatever we want to do, as long as we feel we have the skills to do it, and we think we heard the Lord for ourselves. The laying on of hands is notably missing from the definition, and so, then, is family accountability. Ministry, as it is seen today, rarely requires any personal submission to authority, accountability to fathers in the faith, or the influence of family pace and endorsement.

Family is a word that organizations now use this year for what last year they called community, and the year before that they called mission, and the year before they called ministry. Even new believers are quickly becoming discontent with the wild use of family terms and family ideas, when it is painfully obvious that underneath it all there is no respect for fathers, no promotion of mothers, no understanding of submitting to one another out of reverence for Christ. Most of us now suspect its use as a fancy, new management tool used to manipulate us toward the "vision."

Justice now belongs only to Westerners who are out to save the whole world from all the inequalities that Westerners have created. Justice no longer belongs to God, because we have ceased teaching about the judgment seat of Christ, and as a result we have taken all judgment back to ourselves. We now rule injustice in this world with our own best ideas of how to rescue, how to redeem, and how to reform everything to our measure of equality. Americans, being especially prone to hubris, are the most guilty in this regard, but not alone in the world. The Church, worldwide, with its obsessions in social justice theory, has now become replaceable by any better run charity.

Here is the good news: all of these words belong to the Kingdom of God, and they are restored to absolute perfection when they are understood there. This means, however, that only those who walk in submission to the basic principles of the Kingdom of God are fit to use them. In the hands of the immature and the earthly-minded they all take on immature forms, and in the hands of the weak and selfish they can even become dangerous. Thankfully, in the hands of those who follow Jesus into the Kingdom of God all of these words become beautiful, and useful, and amazing! If we return to the foundational things and choose to walk in them with a simple, childlike, trust, then we will have no problem with these higher things that belong in Kingdom culture.

I have had to take some time outlining the failures in our use of these terms. I fear that because I drilled into them so specifically that I may be misunderstood as a cynic, but that is not the case here at all. I believe we simply have to be honest with one another about our present culture of weakness and immaturity, or we may not develop the passion to change it. We desperately need all of these beautiful words restored to their correct meaning in our spiritual journey, but they can only be defined by the Kingdom of Heaven, and they can only be beautiful when they are built on the foundations of the Kingdom of Heaven. The only way to restore these words to their rightful place, then, is for each of us to go back to the elementary things of the Kingdom listed, quite clearly, in Hebrews 6:1-3, and rebuild our learning, our entire spiritual education, firmly on top of them as our most treasured lessons.

Let's clearly take up our responsibility in the matter. Our present immaturity is not a case of our collective spiritual wit suddenly taking a vacation. It is not the result of a complicated society, or a chaotic age. Nor is the mystery of our inability to be strong in our walk with God the result of a single bad teaching, or the result of persecution from the world. Our spiritual weaknesses cannot be blamed on the secular media. There is no external cause. We are not a spiritual entitlement society so we will not blame others for our own failures. We certainly cannot blame those who don't know Christ for what we still don't know about him ourselves! We need to place the blame for our weakness where it belongs …

The responsibility has now come down to me.

Join me in making confession. Join me in choosing to change. We have failed to build on the basics of God's word at the very lowest levels of our lives, and therefore we have found ourselves failing at many other levels. We need to repent for leaving the simple foundation stones in a chaotic pile of rubble, as we have tried to move on and construct beautiful buildings of faith without them. We, as the responsible members of the community of faith, need to make a new commitment to the elementary teachings of the Kingdom so that we can enjoy a safe and wonderful Church together. I have had to repent as well. I have, at times, lost sight of the goal of the eternal. I have, on more than one occasion, lost my grip on the simple things of faith in Christ. My prayers and repentance on all these matters have been leading me to the conclusions that I have outlined in this book for you: we all need to go back and learn and memorize the elementary things of the Kingdom once again.

We all need to return and impart confidence to one another in these simple building blocks, all resting on Christ, once again. The time is right now, and the people who need this foundational blessing are those within our influence—starting with our own families. Let's find others who will travel with us in this simple, ground-level reconstruction because we will need comrades. We can grow stronger in our faith when we walk with others who love the taste of God's goodness. Soon, we might be able to go on and teach higher-level things like the art of reconciliation, suffering as transformation, generosity as spiritual warfare, and the economy of submission, but first we have to choose to make the first things first.

It is time to choose.

It is time to go deep in the simple things.

Let's pray together like this:

Jesus, I receive you the Christ, the only savior of the world, and I put all of my trust in you. I fall on you as my

Chief Cornerstone and the very foundation of my life. I have no source but you, and no life but in you. I receive all of your words as true, and I know you are fully God and that you have fully expressed God's heart for me. When you became a man on this earth you, single-handedly, through your death, burial, and resurrection became my only path to eternal life and into the presence of my Father in heaven. Your judgment is perfect and your requirements are just.

Jesus, I now turn away from dead works, the kind of works that are sourced from my efforts and from the logic of this world. I choose to turn away from my own attempts at being righteous and throw myself onto you and receive only the righteousness that comes from you. I repent for looking to worldly powers and worldly ways as my source for life and happiness, and I choose to find my source in you. I am no longer from this earth, but you have miraculously transported my life and my citizenship into the eternal realm, and from there I live from now on.

Father, I place all my trust in you. I shout it aloud, "You are always good!" I will proclaim in front of the enemies of this truth that I stand firm in my belief that you always love and that you are always good. I have set all my trust for my life, for my health, for my family, and for my future firmly inside of you, alone. I do not trust my works, or my own mind, or in mystical powers. I do not trust in religion, or in my upbringing, I only trust in you, and in you alone.

Father God, I trust that you can choose your words wisely. I affirm, this day, that you are capable, as God, of choosing your words and guarding them to this day for my benefit. I receive the Bible as your words to me and I submit to all of them. I submit myself to the Scriptures to be conquered by them, and forgive me when I have tried to conquer them. I will read your words and memorize them so they become treasures in my heart, and the preferred language of my mouth. I receive all the promises you have made in your word to me.

Holy Spirit, I receive your baptism. I want to be immersed in you and to live totally in Christ. Jesus, I submit out of obedience to you to be baptized in water, in public, to proclaim your lordship in my life. I have no life, but my life in you. I have turned away from my old life, and I have received your miraculous promise of rebirth into a new, heavenly life in you. I have been baptized into you Father, into you Jesus, and into you Holy Spirit, and am deeply moved by your love to take me in. Holy Spirit, I receive your power to live in Christ, to live righteously, and in you I have all the tools for helping others, living in health, and living victoriously!

Lord Jesus, I receive your invitation into the lineage of God. I have received my adoption into your family, and I have received you, Holy Spirit, as the very substance of my adoption. As a result of my new family connections I will walk, and talk, and dream as a member of a family. I will honor my family, and I will wait on my family to approve me, to celebrate me, and to help assign me to responsibilities. I submit to the Kingdom way of the laying on of hands to give me authority, to bless me with spiritual gifts, and to commission me into confident places of service. I no longer look to organizations or my own resume to give me confidence, but I seek out sweet relationships of trust to establish me in your family and in my perfect fit in your body.

Thank you, Jesus, that I am going to have a new body! Thank you that my grief over death and loss of those I love is coming to an end because you have conquered death and shared that victory with me. I will not place all my hopes for safety and preservation and health on this earthly body because it is my home for only a short while. I do not love the world, as beautiful as it is, as much as I love the next world where in my new, heavenly body, I can enjoy your presence and enjoy eternity with you and all those you love alongside me.

Praise you Lord for eternal judgment. As hard as it is for my intellect I have already affirmed my unwavering trust in your goodness and I have no doubt in your plans. If you have said it, then it is so, and it is just, and it is eternally right. I look forward to the Judgment Day when I will stand before you and give an account of my life. I know you will set everything perfectly right! May it please you to judge me, and may you find many eternal works in my life to reward, and few dead works, where I lived with no faith, that bring you no pleasure. Thank you God for the final judgment of the unrighteous because in it your plans are just, and your plans are righteous and good. You, Holy God, will have your way with all of your creation, it belongs to you, and I submit to your way in everything, even the final judgments. I look forward to the next age with you, and have placed all my longings there with you in your eternal Kingdom.

Amen.

AFTERWORD

On a personal note, I thought it would be kind to explain that everything I have written in this short book is not yet a comfortable fit in my personal wardrobe, either. I have written on what I believe to be a few of the most clear teachings in the Scripture, but it is difficult for me to wrap some of them around my life as well. What I have not meant to imply is that I expect every believer who reads these teachings to jump to attention, agree with me on every point, and immediately practice every challenge I have made. That would be hypocritical of me, since I am making awkward progress on some of them myself. That being said, I do expect something from you. It is the same thing I expect from myself, so this is a respectful expectation.

I expect you to *lean*.

When I know that God is challenging me in a new direction the least I can do is lean toward it. I may not understand why he is dealing with me in a certain way. I may not know exactly where this new direction will lead me, but if I know that God is leading then I can at least lean toward his leadership to practice my trust in him. Leaning is the process of shifting our weight in the direction we intend to go. My sons jump on the trampoline all the time—I mean, all the time. Their obsession has taught them a lot of things about balance and direction that I may otherwise have never known. One thing they have shown me is that wherever you point your head is the direction your body will want to go. So, to perform a front flip they jump, tuck their head in toward their belly buttons, and, amazingly, they land the front flip! They have also figured out that when jumping really high on the trampoline, the slightest tilt of their head can take them on a brand new course, so they choose to be carefully aware of their posture at all times.

I am expecting that each of us will tilt our heads toward the teachings from Hebrews 6. Right thinking leads to right action, so even the slightest motion we make with our heads toward the elementary teachings of the Kingdom can bring about significant change in our direction with God. I am expecting each of us to lean toward the most simple foundations in following Jesus. I believe that if we do this, that we will begin to move with God toward the dreams he has for all of us. Whether we understand everything perfectly or not, I believe we still must lean. Even if we can't predict every implication of these simple teachings, I still believe we should lean toward them, and then allow our lives to follow.

I can also say, to encourage you, that I have faced these lessons in very practical and difficult ways in my own life. My first draft of this book had tons of examples from my own life and of people I know as we attempted to embrace or deflect the weight of these teachings. I removed them to make the book speed along faster, and to avoid narrowing each teaching's application to a single example from my experience. I decided to fly over the teachings with a bit more altitude so you could get the broadest view possible in such a short book, and understand how broadly they can be applied to everyday life. I relay this to you so you understand that, for me, this is not a philosophical work cooked up in an academic research room. These struggles have been on display in the arena of my life, and in some cases the arena, as it were, also contained lions and gladiators.

I still remember where I was the first time I was challenged to forgive God for disappointing me. I remember that it felt almost sinful to consider such a thing, but I did it anyway because I knew I wanted to restore a trust in the goodness of God's heart. I was learning to place my faith in God, and it was hard. I can also remember the first time someone asked me if I had been baptized in the Holy Spirit, and how the feelings that came up in me could only be described as rage. I had cultivated an extreme kind of self-defense around the idea of truth as a young believer, and challenges to my theological rightness felt like an attack on the core of my safety in God. The instructions about baptisms caused me some serious difficulty, at much deeper levels than arguing about whether to sprinkle or immerse. I can also remember the first time I entertained the company of Church leadership who did not wear their denominational affiliations as the brightest part of the name badge on their lapel. This made me feel very, very suspicious, because membership in an established religious institution seemed to be required at the very ground level of legitimacy in my Christian world-view. Receiving the Kingdom way of the laying on of hands was not natural to me at all. I also remember the first time I tried to explain to my own father what I had been learning at college about the mythologies in the Old Testament, and how we had to get past the literal part of the stories so we could discover what God was really trying to say. As I repeated what I had been hearing in my Religious degree program, I felt a kind of odd shame come over me as my father couldn't control his look of disbelief in what I was saying. It took quite a while for me to regain a sense of intellectual confidence in the Scriptures after that season of collegiate "learning." Choosing to trust God at his Word has been very a long, difficult process for me. I cited all these things from my life to show that neither my

Christian tradition, nor my personal practice, have always been in line with the elementary teachings from Hebrews 6. Changing your mind, no, let me correct that, changing my mind is a very difficult thing to do. I have taken many years to lean toward agreement in these simple teachings we have been reading together, and I am still choosing to lean in today.

I first met Bob Terrell back around 1990, or so, and it was his team of leaders that first handed me written teachings on this passage of Scripture from Hebrews. I still have it today. It is a crude photocopied set of paper stapled in the upper left hand corner. Though written previously, it was compiled by Renee Brown for a pastor's training conference on March 3, 1992, and it was entitled the Foundation Series. I rediscovered it in the spring of this year, shoved deep inside a file cabinet drawer. I found it because of a recent conversation I had with Doug Roberts who was part of that team of teachers and prophetic ministers I met along with Bro. Bob, as everyone called him, back in the early 90's. I was telling Doug about how disappointing it was to watch some of my closer comrades collapse under pressure in their spiritual lives. I had been watching a strange assortment of issues rise up and become divisive in relationships with people I knew very closely. I had witnessed, in recent days, people being offended at the commissioning of healthy leadership, because the very idea of Christian leadership had offended them. I had seen people cling to license, like the permission to use recreational drugs, instead of holding on to their faith in God, and the family of faith around them. I had seen people become engrossed in New Age experiments, and self-guided paths to leadership positions, with no respect for the relational foundations of the Church. In moments where the Kingdom process and the Biblical solution would have led to peace and family health, instead there was a devolution into fear, name-calling, and isolation. These situations, among others, really had me off balance. It was a harsh education to see how quickly people can fragment under pressure, and it shocked me more because I knew these folks, personally. What was even more difficult was hearing how justified they were in every decision. They were all extremely confident that their judgments were righteous.

When I relayed these instances to Doug, he shared some of his experiences and insights with me. At one point he said, "Ben, a lot of the time when I have seen people failing under pressure it is because they didn't have a strong foundation. You might need to ask God if you have failed to lay the basic foundations of Christ in the people around you, because it sounds like this may be what God is trying to show you." When I hung up the phone I began to write on the blackboard in my office and process aloud in prayer. I wrote out the things that I thought were basic foundational teachings, and I was asking the Holy Spirit to show me which ones I may have neglected to encourage in the lives of the precious people I watch over. As I was writing I had a eureka moment as Hebrews 6 came to mind, and I began to consider each of those elementary teachings. I began to consider whether or not I had placed them as foundation stones in my sphere of influence. That's when I remembered the old resource file of teachings I had saved from my earliest experience with Bro. Bob and Foundation Ministries. When I finally found the old, photocopied and stapled-up teaching sets, I couldn't believe how much time they spent teaching from Hebrews 6:1-3, and how important each of their Scripture notes were in my own process. My mind was coming alive to the elementary things of the Gospel again, and I began to repent for having neglected to teach the more fundamental things to those I love.

It's true, I had been to tossing around some of the bigger ideas of Kingdom living like: sonship, kingdom, community, grace, etc., with many of my friends, and we had become quite good at it, but these ideas did not build the strength we all really needed. It was not because these higher ideas were not excellent in the Kingdom of God, it was because we didn't have the simpler foundation stones underneath them all, and so, we were not understanding their true Kingdom meaning. To be clear, it was not the mistakes in judgment other people might have made that broke my heart, it was their willingness to devalue their relationships in order to hold to their opinions. People make mistakes all the time, and people have disagreements, but it is a flaw in a person's foundation that would lead them to diminish their family connections as the result. As a family of believers we must always choose to build our relationships on better things like honor, trust, and commitment instead of agreement, permission, and endorsement. We must choose the values that are more valuable to the Kingdom family's health over other self-preserving values. But, we will not have the courage to make this choice if our lives are not built on a strong foundation. When there is weakness in our foundations with Christ, I have now learned, relational challenges and difficult situations will send us running toward our old instincts for self-preservation and self-protection.

I am sure that my wife and I don't agree about everything, but we are still deeply in love, and we are still married after twenty years of disagreements! This is because we have placed the values of honor, trust, and commitment higher than other values in order to prefer one another. My understanding of the relational nature of the Kingdom has become so deeply embedded in me over the years that the very thought of a single disagreement causing a major relational rift just shocks me. It shocked me each time I watched it happen, and it threw me way off balance in my self-view, and my view of others as well. I slowly, through suffering, came to the realization that it was my neglect of these foundational things from Hebrews 6 that had set me up for these relational surprises. This harsh education showed me that I could never assume that because I see these Kingdom foundations in my own imagination, that anyone else in my influence would see them the same way—even if we had spent a lot of time together. This is why Paul told Timothy, "Patiently correct, rebuke, and encourage your people with good teaching. For a time is coming when people will no longer listen to sound and wholesome teaching. They will follow their own desires and will look for teachers who will tell them whatever their itching ears want to hear" (1 Timothy 4:1-3). He didn't tell Timothy to just "hang out with people a lot, and eventually they will get it." He was telling him to relay good teaching, just like the teachings from Hebrews 6:1-3, and to make sure that it was his serious work! I have failed to make these teachings my serious work, and it has cost me dearly. I repent.

In the Kingdom seeking to serve is always better than seeking to lead. Maintaining a healthy position and a good posture with those we influence is so important. It is a privilege to serve others, and a treasure to build strong relationships with the people of God. I hope to never assume anymore on those I love, and I am working to make more honest relational contracts. I want to live in a way that others can quote this Scripture as they think of me, "Dear brothers and sisters, honor those who are your leaders in the Lord's work. They work hard among you and give you spiritual guidance. Show them great respect and wholehearted love because of their work. And live peacefully with each other" (1

Thessalonians 5:12–13). I don't mind telling you that I deeply desire to live at peace with those I influence. I am choosing to work much harder at teaching the elementary things of the Kingdom to those I love, because I think it will help us all live in peace together. Peter felt the same way for every believer, especially leaders, to be kind and respectful to one another, and to learn how to challenge and help each other with humility and grace:

> And now, a word to you who are elders in the churches. I, too, am an elder and a witness to the sufferings of Christ. And I, too, will share in his glory when he is revealed to the whole world. As a fellow elder, I appeal to you: Care for the flock that God has entrusted to you. Watch over it willingly, not grudgingly—not for what you will get out of it, but because you are eager to serve God. Don't lord it over the people assigned to your care, but lead them by your own good example. And when the Great Shepherd appears, you will receive a crown of never-ending glory and honor.
>
> In the same way, you younger men must accept the authority of the elders. And all of you, serve each other in humility, for
> "God opposes the proud
> but favors the humble."
> So humble yourselves under the mighty power of God, and at the right time he will lift you up in honor. (1 Peter 5:1–6).

Would you choose, along with me, to embrace these elementary Kingdom teachings? We could all be transformed toward strength and confidence if these elementary things of the

Kingdom were to become the foundation stones of our lives. If you influence anyone, I mean anyone, would you please share each of these teachings with them as well? If we don't cross these bridges early with those we love, then we are bound to end up in a terrible mix of weakness and misunderstanding. If we want to learn how to grow life-long relationships of depth with our believing comrades, we must circle up around these elementary things, and hold fast to their strength. This book was not designed to be theoretical. This book was designed to teach Kingdom-family principles so we might build more healthy relationships with God and with one another. Relationships of depth are, after all, the most important things in this life, and in the life to come!

So, come along with me. Let's practice Kingdom culture together now, and watch the Father's good heart being poured out all around us! Let's become proficient at the simple things the Father loves, since we will be doing these things, together, for the rest of our eternal lives. For today, at a minimum, let's all choose to at least *lean*.

Jesus asks us to follow him. Many say that a journey begins with the first step. I say that the journey begins, first, with a *lean*. We must shift our weight toward the direction we intend to go before we can even take the first step. Jesus' steps are simple and deep, and we can lean in his direction right now. I believe in you. You can do this. With a simple, childlike trust we can all go on to great things with God, one step at a time. I believe, with all my heart, that if we commit ourselves to the simplest steps in the culture of the Kingdom, our lives, our Church, and our whole community of faith will become more beautiful than we have ever imagined. The transformation will begin in our own lives, and then it will ripple onto the shores of the lives all around us. If you have been holding back on your decision to follow Jesus, I sincerely hope this book has painted a picture so clear, and so wonderful for you, that you know it is time to say, "Yes," to him. If you have been uncertain about whether you could trust God with your whole life, and build your whole life on his basic requirements, I hope this book has given you the encouraging nudge that you have needed to tell God, "I agree with you." It is time for everyone to say "Yes," to God, and live life leaning toward agreement with him.

Go ahead, I'll wait.

www.benpasley.com

CPSIA information can be obtained at www.ICGtesting.com
Printed in the USA
LVOW07s1753301114

416314LV00001B/1/P